TRAINING IN THE ART OF LOVING

GERALD J. AND ELISABETH JUD

Training in the Art of Loving

THE CHURCH AND THE HUMAN POTENTIAL MOVEMENT

A Pilgrim Press Book
Philadelphia

Library of Congress
Catalog Card Number 79-184455

ISBN 0-8298-0223-1

**DEDICATED TO ALL THOSE
WHO SHARED WITH US
IN A SHALOM RETREAT
AND WHO
BY RISKING AND LOVING
HELPED US SHAPE
THE GOOD NEWS REPORTED HERE**

CONTENTS

8 **FOREWORD**

11 **PREFACE**

17 **CHAPTER 1**
A Shalom Retreat
The Environment/Why Do the Retreatants Come?/Who Can Come to the Retreats?/Why Are We Here at Kirkridge Doing This Thing?/Major Hypotheses of Our Research/The Invitation/Basic Principles of a Shalom Retreat/Leadership Style

33 **CHAPTER 2**
The Roots of Shalom Retreats
In Religion's "Cure of Souls"/Roots in the Scientific Study of Groups/Roots in Humanistic Psychology—The Third Force/Growth Centers/Encounter Groups/How Are Shalom Retreats Related to the Human Potential Movement?

47 **CHAPTER 3**
The Components of a Shalom Retreat
Community Building/The Marathon: Some of the Reasons Why We Use the Marathon Method; How the Marathon Is Divided/Primary Methods Used in Shalom Retreats: The Casriel Method; The Encounter Method; Gestalt Methods; Subsidiary Methodologies/Feedback/The Final Morning: Theological Reflections; Celebration

67 **CHAPTER 4**
The Follow-up Study
Introduction/The Research Design: The Groups Under Study; The Research Instruments; The Collecting of Data/Summary of Findings: Basic Data; Behavior Change

85 **CHAPTER 5**
The Follow-up Study (Continued)
Behavior Change—As Indicated by Changes in FIRO-B Scores: Inclusion; Control; Affection/Local Church Relationships: Understanding the Meaning of Life or Religion; The Mission of the Church; Acceptance of the Institutional Church; Celebration; The Importance of Pastors

101 **CHAPTER 6**
Theological Reflections
What They Said/Major Themes: God; Faith and Trust; Love; Church; Community: Freedom/Other Themes/Retelling and Reliving the Biblical Story

117 **CHAPTER 7**
Analysis of Theological Reflections
Introducing Dr. Runyon/Goals of Shalom Retreats/The Context of the Experience: The Enabling Community/The Center of the Experience: Self-affirmation; Guilt, Confession, and Absolution/Fresh Theological Developments: God-language; Identification with the Humanity of Jesus; Exorcism; Experience as an Important Dimmension of Meaning; Tactile Communication/Suggestions: Peak Experience and Continuing Meaning; Social Implications; Sectarianism; Tactile Communication/A Postscript: A Theological Perspective from Germany

137 **CHAPTER 8**
Celebration
Mini-celebrations/The Closing Celebration: The Celebration Is Not a Ritual; How It Begins; The Moods; What Are the Essential Components?; Ecstasy; The Polarity of Joy and Pain; What They Said Months Later; Something to Ponder

151 **CHAPTER 9**
Policy Implications
The Church and the Art of Loving/Community Building/Intensive Experiences and the Biblical Story/Celebration/Relationship of Human Potential Methods to the Local Church/A Shalom Postscript

168 **APPENDIX A**
Retreat Materials

174 **APPENDIX B**
Statistical Tables

188 **APPENDIX C**
Centers Where Human Relations Experiences from a Christian Perspective Are Offered

190 **BIBLIOGRAPHY**

FOREWORD

How "church" reckons with any wide popular movement in the culture can be crucial for all three: church, movement, and culture. This book by Gerald and Elisabeth Jud is especially important in detailing how a creative Christian theologian and his Swiss wife trained in psychology, have brought about a fascinating combination of those same three factors. As readers soon discover, it is a personal, scientific, even historical account of remarkable interest—the more so because here *persons* are being *changed,* sometimes radically and dramatically. At Kirkridge, a retreat-and-study center which has sponsored some of the development (first with caution, then with marveling approval), there is a god-parental enthusiasm about what the Juds have been doing.

One particularly welcome aspect of the situation, and this volume describing it, is the ready parallel discernible between "Shalom retreat" experience and that of Christian "conversion." Characteristics common to old-time "revival" and the Jud groups are evident: the importance of deciding to join the seeking participants, the offer of outgoing love in intensified form, the exploring of murky levels of self-appraisal and unhealth, the exultation of shouting and singing the new wholeness, the opportunity to register publicly that experience, the promise of carry-over into renewed daily living. Like the revival, the Shalom retreat is not necessarily a one-time event, but a renewal which some participants want to share again and again.

However, the incisive difference between the Juds' Shalom retreat and most experiences of "encounter," "human potential," "sensitivity training," or "growth center" therapy, is also the characteristic which separates religious revival from these: a forthright and unargued belief in God. Thus as one looks from face to face in the arms-on-shoulders circle in the "secular" encounter group, there is the sense that all these know, forgive, and uphold each other. After each goes home, there is often a sustaining memory and correspondence, but no more. But in the Shalom group, the I-thou among participants is part of the I-Thou (which Martin Buber himself found to be the basis and end of any person-with-person relation), a personal relatedness within the universe itself. The context is no narrowly held doctrinal claim, but a Christian experience and account of the wholeness of things which the Juds have drawn from the most contemporary and deeply reasoned study of psychology and faith.

This theistic (that is, God-available-as-Person) grounding of the Shalom events is no gimmick or contrived deus-ex-machina device to secure an effect. It comes straight from the Juds' own background and high claim as Christian persons. So for them and members of their "teams," the step which anyone takes to leave his or her hiding place, or the shadows of self-doubt and guilt, is not prompted by a shrewd or sensitive therapist but rather is what *the Lord God* intends. Not only does the Shalom occasion end—as the book pointedly describes—in a period of "theological reflection," but it begins and sustains itself in that same dynamic and serene aura of awareness.

An obvious result of this pervasive "Presence" is the possibility that people may take home with them the continuing access to strength which they have discovered in the Shalom situation. The Hebrew word *Shalom* means more than "peace": it denotes completion, fullness, coming to fruition. As the word is used in farewell, it bids the other person to "Be complete, fulfilled!" And a further meaning is "compassion," the idea being that the filled person has enough grace and to spare, for others. Thus because the Shalom experience here newly links participants up with the caring, ever-steadfast God, it has in many instances been the beginning of a growth and a mission among persons. One of the criticisms often directed at the secular encounter group is that "It just doesn't last . . . " —and the Juds were honestly determined to find how their "alumni" did follow through, using the repeated questionnaires and research techniques mentioned in the book. To the extent that the experience does grow and diversify after the group disperses, it offers new dimensions in the whole field, renewing the retreatant's life with God and providing the continuing strength of that One whom Alcoholics Anonymous members constantly refer to as their "Higher Power."

The felicitous combination of gifts and attitudes which Gerald and Elisabeth Jud demonstrate has not been quickly or easily acquired. Both of them have made it a point to share as fully as possible both the ordinary joys and crises of the day, and the various psychologically astute group processes which have been burgeoning across the country. This odyssey is in some measure like that referred to by Dag Hammarskjold as he said that today the path to sainthood leads "through the world." The Juds have seriously trained themselves, mastered the techniques, opened themselves again and again to the pain and exhaustion and risk of meeting need at deep levels. They have at the same time kept fresh and adaptable their God-among-persons claim. They have brought through with them an increasing multitude of seekers and finders.

The book is a carefully conceived, imaginative, responsible "tract for the times" which can help many people experience or give leadership in the field. That part of the experiment thus far which has taken place at Kirkridge has enlivened our mountaintop even as it has sometimes perplexed hikers along the Appalachian Trail which passes near the retreat house! Like the Juds, we are eager that this very specific account of the whole inspired process may contribute to a radical revitalizing of the churches (which can yet be centers for freeing nonviolent love in the whole culture) and a spiritual deepening of the encounter-group movement which has manifest promise in a time of alienation and fear.

John Oliver Nelson
Jane McTaggart Nelson
at Kirkridge, Bangor, Pennsylvania

PREFACE

Can we learn how to love? Or is love simply something we fall into and therefore something we fall out of just as mysteriously?

It is the intention of this book to answer the former question in the affirmative and to bear witness to a way or ways of helping people love themselves, each other and the world; or to put it another way, to help people hug themselves, each other and the world. We believe we can learn how to love; that impediments to its expression can be removed and its skills taught.

The church talks much of love. The result—people simply feel guilty that they are not able to love properly. You can't teach people to love by talking about it, singing about it or even praying about it. We learn by doing, by interacting, by reflecting and intending.

In a world that has changed drastically, the church has failed to update her style. In our society all major institutions are in trouble. The church is one of these that is behind the times. A hope of the authors is that this book may help in nudging the church to update her style.

As a church executive with primary responsibility for the local church, I (Jerry) have for the past twelve years sought to find the ways whereby the church might assume her full responsibility in helping persons awaken to life and thus release their powers to help build a better world. During these years I have seen the most complicated, dedicated, and surefire methods of rearranging the theological and ecclesiastical furniture come to naught. And I have at length concluded that renewing the church structure is simply not our primary task. A renewed church will emerge when in some deep sense we are a new people; when something equivalent to the early eighteenth-century's Great Awakening stirs us to our roots; when Pentecost is again the common experience of the church.

This book is written by two people who believe that God's

spirit is powerfully present in a movement now sweeping the country. Many people are coming alive in new ways, "turning on." As yet, it is primarily outside of the church as institution and as such what Bonhoeffer would have called "a non-religious experiencing of the Gospel."

Carl Rogers calls it "the most rapidly spreading social invention of the century and probably the most potent. . . "[1] Sam Keen calls it "the soft revolution." He says:

> We are in the middle of two revolutions. One is *hard,* explosive and political. It is concerned primarily with the redistribution of political power and is committed to a strategy of direct confrontation. The other is *soft,* implosive and religious. It is concerned primarily with the alteration of consciousness, with erotic and mystical experience and with the resacralization of intimate relationships. The hard revolution finds its focus in the emergence of power groups—black, brown, student. The soft revolution is diffuse and without organizational manifestations, but its visible outposts are the "growth centers" (now numbering between 90 and 100) which have been modeled on the Esalen Institute in San Francisco.[2]

Both Rogers and Keen are speaking of the Human Potential Movement, a movement which has in some ways affected every major institution in our culture and thousands of people great and small.

The mass media have not missed so important a happening. There it has been praised and criticized, found strikingly worthwhile, and utterly depraved. Generally it is grossly distorted, seen as laden with heavy sexuality, dark violence, and deep forebodings. And usually the important and serious roots of the movement are ignored. This, however, is not always the case. Both in popular press, in journals, and on radio and TV there has been some very sensitive coverage.

One of the major reasons for writing this book is to interpret the movement to churchgoing people to help them to understand that a humanly important movement is underway and that it consists of something other than a few people sitting around naked in tubs, readily jumping in and out of bed with

---

[1]Carl Rogers, *Carl Rogers on Encounter Groups* (New York: Harper & Row, 1970), p. 1.

[2]Copyright 1969 Christian Century Foundation. Reprinted by permission from the December 31, 1969 issue of *The Christian Century.*

one another; that it is instead a movement directly concerned with life and love; with being fully human; with experiencing the transcendent; with realizing our full gifts and making a better world—all serious matters about which Christians and the church should be concerned.

Like every other movement, this movement is made up of many tributaries and includes a wide spectrum of people and ideas. No single tributary is the whole river but the tributaries flow together to make a mighty stream.

The roots of the Human Potential Movement are in the scientific study of groups, the small group movement, sensitivity training, group therapy, sensory awareness, increasing Western awareness of certain Eastern religions, and in humanistic psychology.

There is now appearing in the movement a coalition between religion and humanistic psychology, a new emphasis on the unity of the person (body, mind, and spirit), a new emphasis on the experiential awareness of the self, a new emphasis on the importance of feelings and a new freedom to enjoy feelings, a shift from the Hellenic view of man to the Hebraic, and in the field of human relations a new emphasis on the growth model (entering the future) rather than the sick model (redoing aspects of the past). The leader is seen as a vulnerable person (vulnerability is essential in the leadership style), and love is the context of meeting—a love that cannot be earned.

This book reports the research of two Christians traveling in the Human Potential Movement. Utilizing its methods and joining them with a Christian understanding of the nature of love, we devised a format for retreats lasting from Thursday evening until early Sunday afternoon. We then built a research design to observe and test the results. Our report is mixed with heavy doses of our own enthusiasm and hope, and ends with suggested policy implications for the church.

As a husband and wife we have worked together in this project since its inception. We have worked together as colleagues and peers. It has done us good, strengthened our life together, deepened our love. We both claim full responsibility for the whole book, though each has carried out separate tasks. Elisabeth has had primary responsibility for the follow-up study of retreatants, all the massive correspondence relative to the research, and full responsibility for the computer work. Her labors are primarily reflected in chapters 4 and 5.

On a frontier, we do not wish to make undue claims but we do want to bear our excited witness to what we have seen and heard and felt. We hope the church will listen. If she does not pay attention to this important movement, once again the Master will have come in disguise and the church will have failed to recognize him.

In the course of the book you will read many theological reflections which came out of our retreats. Most of them were written by people who are at least nominally Christian. Here, however, are the words of one outside the church who made no claim to being Christian but who has an important word for us in the churches:

> God is Dead! He died with the witches in Salem—with the oppression of the black man in Georgia—with the slaughter in Cambodia. He died wherever man died in his name! He was murdered by the sanctimonious asses who used his name as venom to poison their own kind. He was used as an instrument of Hate—Death—Destruction by misguided pious bastards who read from the Book what they themselves needed in order to maintain control through fear and oppression.
>
> There is beauty in love. There are those who find that beauty and who work to share it with others. God—like everyone and everything else—can be killed by Hate! But where Hate can kill, Love can heal and every new thing begins with an act of love.
>
> God can begin again if the hearts of men want it, not by direction or mandate—not because of the command to "love God"! God can begin again through love—tenderness—peace—God can begin again if the world finds peace and love in his name instead of hate and destruction.
>
> God can begin again as any life begins—through Love. I hope you make it, God—good luck—If organized religion cares about you at all—they can help—they can help—*not by preaching*—but by *Loving*!!!
>
> There is love in this world and in our hearts—it's been there all the time—but it takes time to find it. This weekend gave us the time to search our hearts—to find love that we never knew was there. It's a beautiful thing, this love.
>
> Please friends—build your churches to honor the love of man—and God will be there. When you build your churches for God—you do so only as a memorial and we all lose—God and man.
>
> Good luck, God. I hope they let you back in again. I'd like to get to know you as a friend.

We have many to thank for help given along the way:

Those who shared with us in Shalom retreats and who provided much of the data for this book. We say with Robert Browning, "I am a part of all that I have met." We met you in the deepest sense of that word and carry you in our hearts.

John Oliver and Jane Nelson, imaginative head and heart of Kirkridge, whose trust encouraged us in this research and who share our hope that this book will be part of Kirkridge's witness to the world.

Theodore Runyon, whose keen and searching mind probed the theological reflections emerging from our retreats and made illuminating commentary.

Marlies Cremer, loved friend from the Bad Boll Academy in Göppingen, West Germany, contributed her love and keen insight.

Clyde Reid, friend and former colleague, made content analysis of the theological reflections.

Howard E. Spragg, executive vice-president of the United Church Board for Homeland Ministries, who encourages his staff to poke around on the frontiers of church and world.

Douglass Johnson and Stanley Haidl of the National Council of Churches who gave time, skill and effort in setting up the appropriate computer program.

Our friend Edward H. Cook, gave us the gift of many hours in reading and rereading the manuscript and in making helpful suggestions.

Willis E. Elliott, theologian, friend, and teacher, greatly improved the manuscript by the generous use of his red pencil.

Rosalind Marshall patiently and faithfully typed the manuscript.

CHAPTER 1

A Shalom Retreat

THE ENVIRONMENT

It is 4 P.M. when we arrive at Kirkridge, a retreat and study center in the Pocono mountains. The meeting place for our retreat is a lodge on a ridgetop overlooking peaceful valleys. The large room in which we meet, glass enclosed, offers a breath-taking view. We are here for a Shalom Retreat and we set to work immediately to shape the environment for the retreat.

Kirkridge is a nondenominational retreat-and-study center founded in 1942 by John Oliver Nelson and some students from Yale Divinity School. Through the years it has been a meeting place for those who picket and those who pray, for Kirkridge is dedicated to bringing the two together. Because Kirkridge is process-oriented and a pilgrim institution, many changes have taken place through the years. If something is well established and well accepted, Kirkridge is not likely to be too interested: it wants to push out the frontiers, break down the dividing walls.

Patterned after Scotland's Iona Community, the various buildings of Kirkridge are named after the neighboring Isles of Iona. The lodge where we meet is called Skerryvore, and the dormitory is called Mull. Only one small building does not have a Scotch name. It is called "Nelson's Folly," and is a one-story building often used by writers who want to get away.

All the meetings of the retreat are conducted in the large room of Skerryvore. Here we encounter, learn to know one another, give and receive love. Here we grow. In a corner of the room we create our place of primary meeting—later to be called by such euphemisms as "the pit," "the salt-mine," and "the altar." Two mattresses are placed in the center, surrounded by other mattresses, placed on simply built folding boards to make the sitting and learning comfortable. Here we will encounter our new friends.

On the walls we place signs and posters, such as:

We are here because there is no refuge
 finally from ourselves.
Until a man confronts himself
 in the eyes and hearts of his fellow men
 he is running.

Until he shares his secret with them,
 he has no safety from it.
He can know neither himself nor anyone else.
 He will be alone.

Where else but in our common ground
 can we find such a mirror?
Here, a man can at last appear clearly to
 himself, not as the giant of his dreams,
 nor the dwarf of his fears,
 but as a man, part of a whole,
 with a share in its purpose.

In this ground we can each take root and grow,
 not alone any more, as in death,
 but alive, a man among men.[1]

A choice that confronts every one of us at every moment is this: shall we permit our fellow men to know us as we now are or shall we seek instead to remain an enigma, an uncertain quantity, wishing to be seen as something we are not?[2]

You cannot love another person, that is, behave toward him so as to foster his happiness and growth unless you know what he needs. And you cannot know what he needs unless he tells you.[3]

Self-disclosure follows an attitude of love and trust. If I love someone, not only do I strive to know him so that I can devote myself more effectively to his well-being, I also display my love by letting him know me. At the same time, by so doing, I permit him to love me.[4]

Encounter is the owning up to your feelings, revealing your here-and-now emotions, no matter how painful, threatening or embarrassing they may be.[5]

And sharing the wall space are these banners:

---

[1]Author unknown. Used in the Synanon Movement.
[2]From *The Transparent Self* by Sidney M. Jourard, p. iii. Copyright © 1964 by Litton Educational Publishing Inc. Reprinted by permission of Van Nostrand Reinhold Company.
[3]Ibid., p. 3.
[4]Ibid., p. 4.
[5]Source unknown.

VULNERABILITY IS THE PATH TO FREEDOM.
LOVE IS INFINITE.
GO INTO ALL THE FUTURE.
HE IS SHALOM.

By 5 P.M. we are ready to greet the first arrivals. Between 16 and 18 persons will participate in the retreat. We prefer to work with 16 but accept 18, counting on an attrition of two. Many times the opposite of attrition occurs and we end up a community of 20. Some will come from long distances, even two thousand miles away, but most will be from nearby states.

WHY DO THE RETREATANTS COME?

They all come seeking something. Some are lonely and seek to overcome the isolation of contemporary life.

Others are hungry for a new life style.

Serious unresolved conflict brings another.

Deteriorating family life leads somebody else to sign up for a retreat.

The crumbling of their belief system motivates yet others.

A hunger for depth experience; a search for identity; hunger for a significant religious experience brings yet some others.

Some are hurting, some are bored, some want to change and believe that the experience here may bring what they want. Some may just be curious. Some come because they want more out of life than they are getting. They want more and don't quite know how to get it.

WHO CAN COME TO THE RETREATS?

The brochure describes what the intent and goals of the retreat are as well as the main methods we use. Persons who are in psychotherapy or long-term counseling are requested to have their therapist's or counselor's permission to participate in the retreat; the same stipulation holds for those who have a history of heart attacks. Married persons are strongly encouraged to attend the retreat with their spouse and those who wish to participate in the retreat alone are strongly urged to bring along a friend. We have found that growth can be seriously slowed or allayed for those who go through this kind of intensive experience alone. When such a person returns home he needs someone to talk to who will understand the experience and who will really be there when the need arises; who will encourage and support him as he tries to put to use what he learned at the retreat and tries to carry out his new intentions. As far as religious affiliation is concerned, we do not require that retreatants be of any particular faith; Jews, Christians as well as nonreligious persons are welcome to participate in a retreat.

WHY ARE WE HERE AT KIRKRIDGE DOING THIS THING?

We are here first of all because our own lives have been significantly affected by the methods which we use in the retreat. We are here because we care about people and because we care about the church and we want to help the church find new ways to enflesh its message of love.

I, Jerry, am a child of Christian nurture. When I was a few days old I was taken into church and I have been there ever since. Much of what I am, my ways of understanding my world, my ways of coping, my ground of hope, I owe to the community of faith which has passed on to me a message about man, the world and God. For seventeen years I was a pastor, doing long- and short-term counseling, leading retreats and group work, and for eleven years I have been an executive in the church system with primary responsibility for the local church. As such I have been aware of the painful position of the church in the new world being born. I know the church is dysfunctional in this culture; that she has failed to update her style fast enough; that her words and her deeds are too often in conflict; that she is geared in her life style to survival culture and not identity culture. And I am much in touch with the pain of our clergy who are caught in the dysfunctioning system.

I have a lover's quarrel with the church but I am inseparably bound to her; bound by birth and covenant. I see myself as part of a pilgrim people who long ago left slavery in Egypt in search of the promised land. So my life is part of a long and rich story. And though the church wanders in the wilderness again and again, I am not without hope for the story of which I am a part had its inception in the wilderness. Even the wanderings are a part of the continuing story. I am a part of what there is of the church today. I own its glory and its shame. And I irritate, agitate, cajole, plead, fight, struggle, urge the church to update her institutional forms and live her life in the right-now world in such a way that she experiences anew and enfleshes the Good News which is her story and the reason for her existence.

I, Elisabeth, in my early years in Switzerland was a nominal child of the church, but in the course of my analysis with Dr. Alphonse Maeder (a colleague of Freud's who broke with him on the subject of religion) I had a significant conversion experience which caused me to see myself as part of the Christian story and to look to the church for nurture. I have been open through the years not only to receive but to give to the church. As I have grown in my pilgrimage I have found this relationship increasingly difficult but I continue to try. Knowing that the central message of the gospel is true, I long with Jerry to help make it plain and to help the church in its task of living and loving.

Both of us see our work as essentially religious in nature. We are not playing games; we are not manipulating methods in order to get people to do what we want them to do. We believe that the methods described in this book are means whereby individuals may get in touch with and release their own powers and thereby become open in a fresh way to God in knowledge, love, and power. (Elisabeth has now resigned her job as clinical psychologist with the Westchester Mental Health Board to work instead in this movement, essentially as a Christian person.)

In recent years we both have been helped in our living by depth experiences in the Human Potential Movement: Jerry by a two-week experience with William Schutz at the National Training Labs in Bethel, Maine; Elisabeth, by a radical experience in a Synanon-oriented marathon at Daytop. Both of us have had training with Dr. Dan Casriel in New York City and have had important learning experiences at Esalen Institute.

Believing that our experience in the Human Potential Movement has an important correlation with the biblical story and at the same time feeling disappointed by the thin interpretation of the meaning of love in our Human Potential experiences, we decided to conduct research in the field, blending Human Potential methodologies and our understanding of the Christian experience of love. Thus we came to approach Kirkridge with our proposition: twelve retreats, each lasting from Thursday evening until Sunday afternoon. We would build a research design relative to the retreats, holding our environment and our methodology steady. When Kirkridge agreed, we had our sponsoring agency and proceeded to build our research design.

MAJOR HYPOTHESES OF OUR RESEARCH

We developed the following hypotheses:

1. By blending the Christian concept of the nature of love and the Human Potential methodologies, we can initiate significant behavioral change in people.
2. The Human Potential methodologies have important implications for community-building in the local church.
3. Intensive experiences utilizing Human Potential procedures can be understood in terms of the biblical story.
4. New concepts (understandings) of celebration can emerge from an analysis of the experiences of Shalom retreats.
5. Persons "turned on" in these experiences can significantly affect the life of their local church.

The methods. We employed methods now commonly available in the Human Potential field. We made our own blending of methods learned from Dr. Dan Casriel, Gestalt therapy, encounter, psychodrama, role play, and sensory awareness. These methods are described in considerable detail in chapter 2.

The data-gathering procedures are as follows:

1. The FIRO-B test, given at the beginning of the retreat and after the passage of at least four months' time. (See chapter 2.)
2. A questionnaire filled out by participants at least four months after the retreat.
3. Also at least four months after the retreat, confidential evaluation of the retreatant by a significant other person.

THE INVITATION

The invitation to the retreats which was broadly distributed included the following information:

> KIRKRIDGE SHALOM RETREATS IN BASIC ENCOUNTER
>
> Through the merging of the ancient Christian witness and new methods of basic encounter, Kirkridge is helping persons to find new hope, new joy and new confidence in life.
>
> It is the business of Kirkridge to be on the frontier. So it is

natural that she should be paying much attention to the human potential movement now sweeping the country. A movement represents the confluence of many tributaries and thus this movement, concerned with the release of human potential, represents the coming together of insights gained from small group work, sensitivity training, group therapy and experiments in heightened sensory awareness. Kirkridge believes that the implications of this movement for the life of the church are great indeed. She is convinced that without solid, caring, loving community at its base, many of the efforts of the local church to make a better society are doomed to fail.

Kirkridge is devoted to Shalom for the structure of society and for the individual person. According to the biblical witness, God's Shalom is the most elementary expression of what life in the new aeon is all about. Jesus leaves Shalom with his disciples, "Shalom I leave with you, my shalom I give unto you (John 14:29)." It stands for peace, integrity, community, harmony, and justice; not just in the structures of society but in the personal life; not just in the head but in the belly.

While healing undoubtedly occurs, these retreats are not presented as therapy for sick people but as a means of releasing the potential for fuller living that is in all of us.

Experience has taught that the meanings and values of a marathon-retreat are best conserved and reinforced when shared. We strongly urge you, if possible, not to come alone.

The retreats begin with dinner on Thursday evening and end shortly after lunch on Sunday.

The schedule includes community building, a 24-hour marathon of continuous encounter, feedback given to each participant by all members of the group, theological reflection and celebration.

BASIC PRINCIPLES OF A SHALOM RETREAT

I. An Understanding of Love from a Christian Perspective

Rollo May in his book *Love and Will* says that

> there are four kinds of love in Western tradition. *One is sex*, or what we call lust, libido. *The second is eros*, the drive of love to procreate or create—the urge, as the Greeks put it, toward higher forms of being and relationship. *A third is philia*, or friendship, brotherly love. *The fourth is agape* or caritas as the Latins called it, the love which is devoted to the welfare of the other, the prototype of which is the love of God for man.[6]

---

[6]Rollo May, *Love and Will* (New York: W. W. Norton & Co., 1969), pp. 37–38.

Then he adds, "Every human experience of authentic love is a blending in varying proportions of these four."[7]

We are much in sympathy with the point of view expressed in this important book. And since it is our purpose here to set down basic working principles of our retreats rather than to make a lengthy defense of them, it is enough to say here that we are much undergirded by the point of view expressed by May in *Love and Will.*

Of the four Western understandings of the nature of love, we derive our understanding primarily from "agape." This is the love described in the hymn of love in 1 Corinthians 13. The early Christians poured into the word agape all their understandings of God's love which had come to them in Jesus Christ; agape comes as a free gift, unearned and unmerited. The response to it is to seek to love one's fellowman in the same way. To experience love is to experience "grace"; to be loving is to be graceful, full of grace, which is agape in action.

The church, of course, has no corner on love but that she has a rich history of understanding its nature, despite following that Way falteringly.

The meaning of love moves into poetry and music, and into mystery. While fully aware of this we simply claim that it can be taken out of the abstract and described in simple operational principles that are easily understood. And we know that the experience of love in its simple form prepares one to pass into its mysteries—into the transcendent.

Here is what we deduce from the Christian concept of love.

1. Each of us is capable of growing in his powers and skills of giving and receiving love. Despite this truth, many die of thirst in a fresh water lake. All about us are those who can give us what we need; we must only learn to ask and then pay up by receiving.

2. Love is an act of the will. It can be intended and is not something into which we fall.

3. Love is an attitudinal stance of good will which we take toward another person.

4. It cannot be earned. Whatever has to be earned is not the real article.

5. It is not time-bound. One does not have to know another

---

[7] Ibid., p. 38.

person for a long time before loving him. "And Jesus looked upon him and loved him (Mark 10:21)."

6. Love is a response to need. You cannot love an un-needy person. Our culture lifts high the virtues of self-sufficiency and independence and those who act as though they need no one receive little love. It is only as we lay bare our needs and open ourselves to receive love that we move from independence to interdependence, the basis of true community.

From our Christian understanding of the meaning of love we have derived the following operational principles:

SEEING

I SEE YOU I do not look over you, under you, through you. I see you there in your uniqueness.	I need to be seen. I want to be seen. SEE ME!

HEARING

I HEAR YOU I listen for the meanings behind your words.	I need you to hear *me*; not just my words. I need you to help me say what I intend and to hear the message behind my words.

FEELINGS AND IDEAS

YOU HAVE FEELINGS AND IDEAS I recognize your right to feel and think as you do. I may not agree with your feelings and ideas but you are entitled to them because you are human.	Only when I fully acknowledge my feelings and ideas can I grow. If in your presence I can be honest and open about my feelings, and ideas, then I can be honest, open and I can grow.

GOODWILL

I HAVE GOOD-
WILL FOR YOU
I will you good and not
evil. I care
about you.

I need your goodwill,
your help and under-
standing, in order to
develop my potential.
Alone I cannot
grow. I need your caring.

NEEDS

YOU HAVE NEEDS
If you disclose them
to me, within the
limitations of my
own value system,
I will not run away. I
will be there for you.

If I am left alone with
my needs, where shall I
turn? I can only deny
having them, stuff them
down or pretend that
they do not exist—or
seek to have them filled
in some devious way. I
need to believe that
when I share my needs
with you, you will not
run away.

The methods used at the retreats provide the opportunity for the retreatants to experience and interiorize the truth of the above principles.

II. The Unity of Body and Spirit

Much of past Christian teaching was burdened with a dualism which held the spirit superior to the body and feelings inferior to the mind. Thus many are ashamed of their bodies and pretend they do not have them, are embarrassed by feelings and tend to suppress them and even to deny their existence.

Our Hebrew and Christian heritages have highlighted the sense of hearing as the channel of salvation: "Hear the word of the Lord, believe and be saved." The other senses have not been denied but relatively neglected.

Now, in our time we have become acutely aware that there are some very important things going on down yonder below our ears. To be fully alive and to fulfill our potential as human beings we need to get in touch with the rest of the body, "listen" to what it is telling us, and use the whole "body"—the whole person—to rejoice before the Lord. We are not simply our bodies but our bodies are part of who we are, part of our total being. "We do not *have* a body, we *are* a body," is a common saying in the Human Potential Movement. We do need to come to our senses, become aware again of touch, smell, taste, hearing, and seeing. Fritz Perls says, "Lose your mind and come to your senses."[8] Judaism and thus Christianity provide important knowledge relative to the body-spirit unity of man. We need to recover this sense of unity.

We are keenly aware of the unresolved theological problems in this area but are convinced that we should re-own the sense of our body: nothing in the Christian faith itself is inimical to this recovery. Accordingly we use many methods which help people achieve this.

III. The Importance of Acknowledging and Expressing Feelings and Needs

We are indebted here to Dr. Dan Casriel. All of us have a deep need to be loved, to be accepted as we are, to have our thoughts, opinions and feelings taken seriously. We want to be seen not simply for what we are but for what we may become. We want others to hear not just what we say but what we try to say; we even want them to help us say it.

But since early childhood we were conditioned (programmed) to hide our feelings, not to express them overtly. Overt expression usually met with disapproval, which made us feel *rejected*, unloved and the accompanying feelings were very painful; so we learned that to avoid the pain, it was wiser to act the way we were expected to act, at least when our behavior could be noticed. We ended up believing that only good feelings such as love, were acceptable.

As a youngster I was punished for expressing anger; so I learned to hide my anger. I was told not to cry when I was hurt; so I learned to hide my pain. I was ridiculed when I was afraid; so I learned to hide my fear. Don't express feelings! Don't be angry; don't cry; don't be afraid! Hide your feelings! Push them down! There are millions of people now who act as if they had no feelings whatsoever; who feel that they are not

---

[8]Frederick S. Perls, *Gestalt Therapy Verbatim* (Lafayette, Calif.: Real People Press, 1969), p. 69.

entitled to their feelings; who believe that anger, pain and fear are in themselves bad; live on flat plateaus, knowing neither the heights of joy nor the depths of anguish and pain.

Most of us have been hurt, have experienced so much rejection that it is understandable if we believe we are not lovable. We were programmed to believe we would lose the respect and approval (a poor substitute for love) of our fellowmen if we let our feelings out; we "play games" in our relationship with other people, wear masks of friendliness when often we are full of resentment and anger.

One of the banners which hangs on the walls at Kirkridge says, "Vulnerability is the path to freedom." It is indeed risky to be one's self, to express one's feelings and needs openly and directly. We do take the chance that we will be rebuffed when we want to express genuine affection toward a person about whom we care. We will not be loved by everyone to whom we express our anger openly; we may be reprimanded for acting "emotional," "immature," nonprofessional, etc. But we stand to lose much more if we do not take that risk.

If we do not express our anger straight, it comes out sideways. We let it out toward our spouse, children or the dog when we come home from work. We may remain preoccupied for days and weeks with a wrong we feel somebody has done us or even an imagined wrong. We may complain to a friend about the injustice we feel our spouse did us or gripe to a fellow parishioner about something we do not like about our pastor's or a fellow parishioner's behavior. We do not express the feeling where it rightly belongs. And at what cost? We end up feeling alienated from those we love and whom we really care about. Communication breaks down. A barrier is erected behind which we hide, nursing our feelings of having been abused. We become depressed, develop tension headaches, or some other physical sign which reveals that we are trying to hide what is really "eating us."

So also with fear and pain. When they are pushed down, they do not leave us. They are impacted in our belly, distort our behavior or punish us for our suppressive maneuvers by giving us physical discomfort of some sort or other. Our body speaks to us and we do not listen. God speaks to us through our body and we do not listen.

In the course of our retreats we try to help people get in touch with their feelings; own them; to express them fully and freely; to feel entitled to such expression; to learn to let them come out straight instead of sideways.

We are all so locked up in ourselves; we have so many defenses going, that we have forgotten how to feel. We are physically tight and it takes a lot of energy to keep the lid on those feelings! We are emotionally so tight that we don't dare to let go for fear of finding out what we really feel. What a relief to get rid of these blocks and then to start growing! We can all learn to take the risk involved in acknowledging and expressing feelings, opening up a little at a time, in a safe situation like a group where all are struggling for greater freedom and more honesty about their feelings. Our retreat methods help this to happen.

Expressing need. Because a person is alive, because he is human means also that he is a needy being. All of us at times are like an empty cup that needs filling. But people differ widely in their ability to bring to the surface their needs. Even when they do they have to deal with feelings of unworthiness, that cause many people to knock themselves out in good works, trying to earn the right to have their needs met and to be loved. They have interiorized Jesus' description saying, "It is more blessed to give than to receive" to mean an imperative that one should constantly be giving—but they also weakly hope that something may trickle back to them. They forget that Jesus also said, "Ask and you shall receive (Matt. 7:7)." So on our retreats we help people to ask, come out straight in asking of life and in asking other persons to meet their needs. If love is a response to need, then it is indeed the needy person, the one who comes out straight with his need, who is more apt to receive that love.

IV. Self-actualization

Abraham Maslow, one of the fathers of the Human Potential Movement, firmly believed that science should study not only the sick but also the well. He believed humans should have as their goal not simply adjustment but transcendence—to be self-actualizing and to aspire to more peak experiences. We are much committed to Maslow's concept of self-actualization. Because we intend that the retreat experience move each person in the direction of self-actualization, we consider it very important that the reader grasp the meaning of this term.

In an important essay called "Self-Actualization and Beyond," Maslow explores some aspects of the nature of self-actualization, in terms of the operational meaning of the self-actualization process. He defines self-actualization as follows:

> *Self-actualizing people are, without one single exception, involved in a cause outside their own skin, in something outside of themselves.* They are devoted, working at something, something which is very precious to them—some calling or vocation in the old sense, the priestly sense. They are working at something which fate has called them to somehow and which they work at and which they love, so that the work-joy dichotomy in them disappears. One devotes his life to the law, another to justice, another to beauty or truth. All, in one way or another, devote their lives to the search for what I have called (1962) the "being values" (B, for short), the ultimate values which are intrinsic, which cannot be reduced to anything more ultimate. There are about fourteen of these B-values, including the truth and beauty and goodness of the ancients and perfection, simplicity, comprehensiveness, and several more.[9]

In the light of Maslow's concept of self-actualization, we seek the following in Shalom retreats:

1. To help the person experience the group life and his own feelings fully, vividly and with full concentration and total absorption.
2. To help the person make the growth choice instead of the fear choice.
3. To encourage one to listen to the impulse voices.
4. To encourage honesty.
5. To help one to move toward responsibility for his own behavior.
6. To help one to move toward deciding what is right for him.
7. To help people to use their intelligence in making their choices and help them to do well the thing they want to do.
8. To set up the conditions for peak experiences and help people to recognize them when they happen.
9. To help persons identify their defenses, and after the defenses have been identified, help them find the courage to give them up.

---

[9]From Abraham Maslow in *Challenges of Humanistic Psychology*, ed. James F. Bugental (New York: McGraw-Hill, 1967) pp. 280–81. Copyright 1967 by McGraw-Hill, Inc. Used with permission of McGraw-Hill Book Company.

LEADERSHIP STYLE

We believe that leadership style is of critical importance and that what happens to people as persons and as a group at our Shalom retreats is strongly influenced by the style of leadership we have chosen. It is characterized by the following:

1. *The "medium is the message."* We try to show ourselves as real people who have lived through some of our own tough problems and are still struggling with ourselves and others. Openness and honesty in interpersonal relations is one of the goals of the retreat, so we try to model this kind of behavior. We fully participate in the dynamics of the retreat, we work always in the process, never stand outside. During those occasions when the group does verbal and nonverbal exercises, we are fully participant and attempt to reveal ourselves as well. We seek to be vulnerable, not only allowing but encouraging persons to express their feelings, positive and negative, toward us. And when an impasse arises in the group, we do not run away from it but deal with it as openly and in as straightforward a fashion as we can.

2. *Releasing the latent power of the group to heal, help, and love produces the apparent miracle of the retreat.* The release of that great power is one of our major intentions. From the beginning we emphasize that we all have much to give and to receive from one another. We set out to promote interdependency rather than dependency only upon the leaders and encourage people to get involved with each other as fully and as soon as possible. We feel it is important for all to have the experience that they can help other people by being present to them; that they need not depend on the "experts" to bring about healing.

3. *Openness to receive.* We are in touch with our own need for love and we express this need openly toward other members of the group. Thus we are not just givers but very much receivers of love. At the end of each retreat we feel very strongly that our cup has been filled too. Apart from being physically tired, we do not feel sucked on or drained.

4. *Man-woman team advantages.* It seems clear to us that there are great advantages to being a man-woman team. The gifts male and female have to give differ, and differ also according to the sex given to. Often one of us is better able to empathize with a person out of his own experience while he

may get stuck dealing with a situation which is totally foreign to his experience.

For example: out of Jerry's working through intense grief he can especially be present to a person struggling to come to terms with a similar experience; on the other hand, Elisabeth, who lived for many years as a single woman, knows from her own experience what it feels like to live alone.

5. *In charge of process.* The retreats have a very clear-cut process. At the beginning of the retreat we discuss the process with the group. We make a contract about it. Then we remain faithful to it. As early as possible we share leadership with the group but the process does not change.

6. *Teaching from inside the experience.* We believe that the experience is indeed the best teacher. But from time to time during the living out of the experience, we pause either to interpret the process or to illumine the experience by referring to some important biblical story or truth. We use this device to help people awaken to the rich storehouse of wisdom in the Bible when it is seen not as a belief bag in which we are entrapped but as light to help us understand the here and now.

CHAPTER 2

The Roots of Shalom Retreats

We find the roots of Shalom retreats in the long history of religion's "Cure of Souls," in the scientific study of groups, in humanistic psychology as a Third Force, and in the development of growth centers.

IN RELIGION'S "CURE OF SOULS"

What is going on at Kirkridge in Shalom retreats is part of the long history of the church's concern for the spiritual growth and development of man. The church, of course, did not invent groups meeting for growth purposes. Such groups are probably as old as man himself. But the institution of religion has always made some use of groups for learning and growing.

Jesus and his disciples left the crowded city and went into the countryside to talk and to pray. The early followers of Jesus gathered in each others' homes to be strengthened in their faith and love long before the church was made legal. Such gatherings bore the marks of the small group movement. Priests in parishes and monks in monasteries have through the ages made rich use of this form of human experiencing. John Wesley during the eighteenth-century revival developed a sophisticated form of group work. And among the Christian communal experiments in the United States during the nineteenth century, early forms of what goes on now at Kirkridge, were already practiced. Meetings of the Oneida Community, for example, show a remarkable similarity to encounter group sessions.

One of the more recent precursors of what happens at Shalom retreats is the Oxford Group Movement, also called Moral Re-Armament. This group was founded in the 1930's by Frank Buchman, the secretary of the Student Christian Association in State College, Pennsylvania, a small university town. The Movement has as its goal the "changed" life, by which it means conversion, the reorientation of the individual toward a better life. Quite intensive group methods, emphasizing confession to the group, are being utilized in the groups. The group sees its world mission in terms of changing people rather than in changing political situations, social structures, or economic systems.[1] The group tends to draw many people who are interested in the religious life but unfortunately are also deeply committed to the maintenance of the status quo. Though we share with the Oxford Group the concern about change, the maintenance of the status quo is quite the opposite of what we intend. The unjust structures which serve as prisons for many must be replaced. We want to help people to grow in love and to release people's potential to work in the process of making a better world.

A further indication of religion's historic concern in this field is in the area of training for the ministry. For many years students preparing for the pastoral ministry have been trained in counseling. And as a result, even though too often an unholy alliance has been made with Freudianism, the church has been plainly involved in the healing ministry. While this has been a great strength, the weakness has been that the emphasis has been too little on the healing powers of the community of faith and love and too much centered in the pastor (therapist).

In the early 50's the Small Group Movement emerged with power in the church. It was fueled by the scientific study of groups which was at that time also beginning to have powerful impact. Drawing on the rich heritage of the church's concern for persons, it intensified group life in many churches and gave many Protestants powerful experiences of warmth and intimacy together with renewed insights into their faith. Kirkridge was one of the outposts of this movement and its impact on the life of the church has been strong.

The Episcopal Church was among the first of the major denominations to take an interest in the sensitivity training movement and for a number of years sponsored its own program for church leaders with the staff trained at the National Training Laboratories at Bethel, Maine. Now most of the major denominations have programming in this area. The

---

[1]Cf. Walter Houston Clark, *The Oxford Group* (New York: Twayne Publishers, 1951), p. 27.

National Council of Churches for a number of years has offered management training courses in Washington, D.C. and leadership training at Green Lake, Wisconsin. These courses have made much use of the insights emerging from the scientific study of groups.

Now the emergence of the Human Potential Movement promises to initiate another rich period of growth in the church's long history of concern for souls.

Whereas the field of religion has its own unique task to perform, it is important that it form alliances with any who have something to teach concerning man and the means whereby his potential is released.

James V. Clark holds a doctorate in business administration in organizational behavior from Harvard University School of Business. He is associate professor of business administration at the University of California. Here is what he has to say about sensitivity training and religious development:

> I am engaged in the practice of working as a professional in so-called sensitivity training groups. More recently these are coming to be called "basic encounter" groups and the term has much merit, for the longer I work in such settings, the more I see man as grappling with and toward some of the most profound aspects of his existence. Specifically (and very much to my surprise, for I had rejected organized religion like many other intellectuals), I have discovered for myself how deep man's needs for religious experience are. *Time and again I have seen persons unfold in a way that has forced me to conclude that sensitivity training is indeed a religious enterprise. I am even more surprised to find myself thinking IT IS THE MOST RELIGIOUS ENTERPRISE OF WHICH I KNOW.*
>
> Placed in the environment of one of these groups, people seem, in their own ways to go through the development of a religion. Although the revelations and the symbols used in each individual's faith and witnessing have their own unique content for each person, the process each person goes through appears similar to the development of any religion. It is thus the case that sensitivity training offers both a technology for the creation of meaningful religious development and an unparalleled laboratory for the study of the necessary elements of religious experience.
>
> It is in this sense then, that those concerned with religious development can find in this new growth-oriented technology of sensitivity training a surprising ally. There is reason to believe that the pedagogy of religious experience has advanced far beyond what many religionists are aware of.
>
> And finally, I hope that my colleagues in the practice of

sensitivity training can come to see that organized religion is not inherently and irrevocably anti-religious as they may have thought. WHAT WOULD OUR SOCIETY LOOK LIKE IF EVERY CHURCH AND TEMPLE IN AMERICA CENTERED AROUND ENCOUNTER GROUPS? SUCH A VISION IS POSSIBLE, I KNOW, FOR WHENEVER I HAVE CONDUCTED SENSITIVITY TRAINING EXPERIENCES FOR RELIGIOUS ORGANIZATION LEADERS, THEY HAVE COME TO SEE VIVIDLY THE PROFOUND RELEVANCE OF SENSITIVITY TRAINING FOR THEIR LIFE AND WORK. TIME AND AGAIN THESE GROWTHFUL AND HUMBLE PEOPLE, BISHOPS, PRIESTS, MINISTERS AND THE LIKE HAVE TOLD SENSITIVITY TRAINING PROFESSIONALS THAT IN THESE GROUPS THEY HAVE SEEN CHRIST AND GOD IN WAYS THEY NEVER THOUGHT POSSIBLE.

They have seen him where Martin Buber told us to look, between man and man. They have seen Him where Paul Tillich told us to look, in our own depths. But they have seen Him because they were in an educational experience in which they could face one another and reveal their beingness. The existence of such an educational experience is good news indeed.[2]

After spending a year studying the Human Potential Movement, exposing herself to its methods and spirit, Jane Howard wrote a book called *Please Touch*. Toward the end she writes of her own falling away from the church and of the eschewing of the church by her generation. But then she concludes, "The Human Potential Movement, however, has made me think that if the churches really wanted to, they could lure us back for a second look. A massive mutual transfusion is now in progress between organized religion and sensitivity training."[3]

Shalom retreats have their roots deep in the history of religion. So at Kirkridge we are about the ancient business of the church but with a new ally.

ROOTS IN THE SCIENTIFIC STUDY OF GROUPS

Since the early 1950's the church has been much helped by the insights emerging from the scientific study of groups. We still have much more to learn.

---

[2]From James V. Clark in *Challenges of Humanistic Psychology*, ed. James F. Bugental (New York: McGraw-Hill, 1967), p. 258. Copyright © 1967 by McGraw-Hill, Inc. Used by permission of McGraw-Hill Book Company.

[3]Jane Howard, *Please Touch* (New York: McGraw-Hill, 1970), p. 213.

In the 1880's a German sociologist by the name of Ferdinand Tonnies made a distinction between *Gesellschaft* (an impersonal bureaucratic hierarchy) and *Gemeinschaft* (a closer, more personal community). He is often seen as the father of the scientific study of groups. Sometime later J. J. Moreno organized prostitutes into a trade union and began in his work with them the early use of psychodrama.

Deeply motivated to learn the means whereby self-help groups might learn to avoid the evils of totalitarianism he had experienced, Kurt Lewin, a famous psychologist, came to the United States from Nazi Germany. All students of group dynamics look to him as a seminal thinker. He believed that training in human relations was an overlooked type of education. He developed the concept of "Force Field Analysis" which sets forth the belief that events are determined by immediate forces rather than distant ones. He believed that behavior could be changed if people could identify which forces restrained them from desirable action and which ones drove them toward it. He was the founder of the Research Center for Group Dynamics at MIT.

Interest in the scientific study of small groups received its greatest impetus from groups of educators and scientists who gathered at Bethel, Maine in the late 40's. They developed the National Training Laboratories at Bethel in 1954. Leland Bradford, then director of the Adult Education Division of the National Education Association became the founder of what is now referred to as NTL (National Training Laboratories). Ronald Lippitt, now of the University of Michigan and Kenneth Benne, now of the Boston University Human Relations Center were his collaborators in developing the first T-groups (T=training). It was their conviction that such training laboratories could teach far more effectively than lectures. Through the influence of NTL, human relations training began to take hold in industry and later in many other institutions; it is still going strong.

Since Bradford, Benne, and Lippitt came from the fields of education and philosophy, the sociology of groups rather than the psychology of groups was the primary emphasis in the early years of the movement; the roles and functions of leadership and membership in groups, rather than the growth of the individual. But parallel to this movement other developments were beginning to take shape. At about the same time as

NTL was being formed, Carl Rogers at the University of Chicago was involved in training personal counselors for the Veterans Administration. During this process he and his staff experimented with intensive group experiences during which the trainees

> met for several hours each day in order to better understand themselves, to become aware of attitudes which might be self-defeating in the counseling relationship, and to relate to each other in ways that would be helpful and could carry over into their counseling work. This was an attempt to tie together experimental and cognitive learning in a process which had therapeutic value for the individual.[4]

Rogers further describes this important development:

> The Chicago groups were oriented primarily toward personal growth and the development and improvement of interpersonal communication and relationships, rather than having these as secondary aims. They also had more of an experiential and therapeutic orientation than the groups originating in Bethel. OVER THE YEARS THIS ORIENTATION TOWARD PERSONAL AND THERAPEUTIC GROWTH HAS BECOME MERGED WITH THE FOCUS OF TRAINING IN HUMAN RELATIONS-SKILLS, AND THE TWO COMBINED FORM THE CORE OF THE TREND WHICH IS SPREADING SO RAPIDLY THROUGHOUT THE COUNTRY TODAY.[5]

The movement for the scientific study of groups goes on unabated. The small stream has grown into a mighty river that has penetrated education, industry, church, and practically every other major institution.

ROOTS IN HUMANISTIC PSYCHOLOGY—THE THIRD FORCE

The field of psychology in America has been dominated by two forces, behaviorism and Freudianism. But in recent years a "third force" has emerged and it is with this third force that Shalom retreats are essentially identified. Scholars related to this area of psychology say that man must be seen as a whole and therefore they resist any approach which reduces the behavior of man to quantitative terms. They also reject as destructive the Freudian approach which contents itself with

---

[4]Carl Rogers, *Carl Rogers on Encounter Groups* (New York: Harper & Row, 1970), p. 3.
[5]Ibid., pp. 3–4.

exploring the inner recesses of consciousness, in favor of instilling a higher human awareness or "self-actualization."

James F. Bugental, one of the important leaders of the movement, says:

> I have very clearly taken sides in this issue between the objectivist and subjectivist approaches to the study of man. I sincerely believe this is such a conflict as may well be termed a battle for man's soul. It is so not because behaviorism is following a blind alley but because it is clearly effective within its frighteningly limited perspective. Paul Tillich said, "Man resists objectification, and if his resistance to it is broken, man himself is broken."
>
> To put the point quite starkly, it makes a very great difference to the world of man and to man's own experience of his life which view of his nature and which orientation to the study of his being is dominant.[6]

Then he proceeds to show how the humanistic orientation differs from the behavioristic in a number of ways.

> *The humanistic psychologist:*
> 1. Disavows as inadequate and even misleading, descriptions of human functioning and experience based wholly or in large part on subhuman species.
> 2. Insists that meaning is more important than method in choosing problems for study, in designing and executing the studies, and in interpreting their results.
> 3. Gives primary concern to man's subjective experience and secondary concern to his actions, insisting that this primacy of the subjective is fundamental in any human endeavor.
> 4. Sees a constant interaction between "science" and "application" such that each constantly contributes to the other and the attempt rigidly to separate them is recognized as handicapping to both.
> 5. Is concerned with the individual, the exceptional, and the unpredicted rather than seeking only to study the regular, the universal, and the conforming.
> 6. Seeks that which may expand or enrich man's experience and rejects the paralyzing perspective of nothing-but thinking.[7]

Reflecting the power of the growing movement, the Association for Humanistic Psychology was formed only a few years ago. Here is its own description:

> "Humanistic Psychology" is a name applied to a broad spectrum

---

[6]From *Challenges of Humanistic Psychology,* ed. James F. Bugental, op. cit., p. 9.
[7]Ibid.

of approaches to human experience and behavior, all of which depart in their own ways from the traditional emphases of behaviorism and psychoanalysis and are now in the process of becoming affiliated into a loose unity. The Association for Humanistic Psychology (originally American Association for Humanistic Psychology) was formed in 1962 to provide a meeting place for professional psychologists and others who share a commitment to the fundamental uniqueness and importance of human life. Perhaps most important are the convictions that all human beings are basically creative and that intentionality and values are basic determinants of human action.

Although exponents of the humanistic orientation vary widely and often hold conflicting views, the following four characteristics appear as common elements, although even with these there is less than unanimity:

—A centering of attention on the experiencing *person*, and thus a focus as the primary phenomenon in the study of man. Both theoretical explanations and overt behavior are considered secondary to experience itself and to its meaning to the person.

—An emphasis on such distinctively human qualities as choice, creativity, valuation, and self-realization, as opposed to thinking about human beings in mechanistic and reductionistic terms.

—An allegiance to meaningfulness in the selection of problems for study and of research procedures, and an opposition to a primary emphasis on objectivity at the expense of significance.

—An ultimate concern with and valuing of the dignity and worth of man and an interest in the development of the potential inherent in every person. Central in this view is the person as he discovers his own being and relates to other persons and to social groups.

The Association identifies with a broad conception of scientific method and is therefore open as to what may be relevant approaches, methods, or significant aspects of human functioning suitable for exploration. It is fundamentally committed to psychology as a science, rejecting only those philosophical suppositions which restrict the field of inquiry and interfere with a total view of human experience. As a consequence of this orientation, the Association encourages attention to topics having little place in existing systems, such as love, creativity, spontaneity, play, warmth, ego-transcendence, autonomy, responsibility, authenticity, meaning, transcendental experience, courage.[8]

There are many important leaders in the humanistic psychology field. But we want to describe briefly here some who have had the greatest influence upon us both in the development of

---

[8]Association for Humanistic Psychology flyer (416 Hoffman Street, San Francisco, California 94114). Used by permission.

our theory and practice. Their works are listed in the appendix. Here we simply mention them and a central aspect of their work.

Eric Berne focuses on "games" we play with each other. His *Games People Play* was on the best-seller list for over two years. He developed a form of therapy called transactional analysis.

Bernard Gunther was first a student of Charlotte Selver, who originally brought the sensory awareness movement to this country from Germany. He has been an outstanding leader in popularizing the sensory awareness movement and in developing innovations. He is on the Esalen staff.

Thomas A. Harris is director of the International Transactional Analysis Association. He developed and popularized Berne's theories of *Games People Play*. His book *I'm Ok, You're Ok* is very useful to our retreatants when they go home because it gives them an understandable typology for appraising and then modifying their behavior.

Abraham Maslow insisted that science should study not only the sick but the well also; that human beings should go beyond adjustment and attempt to transcend—to be self-actualizing and aspire to peak-experiences. He also showed that our perception of what people need colors our assumptions about human behavior.

To *O. Hobart Mowrer* must go much credit for the discovery of group-methods in psychotherapy. He studied reasons underlying the failure both of religion and psychiatry. During the course of his work he rediscovered some of the truths which the church had used effectively but had allowed to fall into disuse—the use of confession as a group experience, the need for restitution and change in behavior. He was one who early encouraged Kirkridge to pay attention to the Human Potential Movement.

Herbert Otto was for a long time the director of the Human Potentialities Research Project at the University of Utah. There he made a study of resources people possess, what their unused abilities are, hidden strengths. He has developed many methods which are helping people become aware of and develop their potential.

Frederick S. Perls is the originator and developer of Gestalt therapy, an existential approach which combines individual and group therapy. During the last years of his life he was related chiefly to Esalen Institute. The immediate aim of Gestalt therapy is the restoration of awareness at the points of growth impedance—thus Perls's famous line, "Have you discovered something?" Its ultimate goal is the restoration of functions of the organism and the personality which will make an individual whole and release his potentialities.[9]

Carl R. Rogers for 35 years has been a leader in the field of individual counseling and psychotherapy. Known for the development of client-oriented counseling, he is now predominantly interested in the strength of the changes in attitudes and behavior which can be achieved in a group.

William C. Schutz, psychologist, research scientist, and pilgrim spirit, is one of the charismatic leaders of the Human Potential Movement. He is the originator of the FIRO tests, and popular author of *Joy*. He has just completed a new manuscript describing various aspects of his work entitled "Here Comes Everybody." He is describing among other things the psychosomatic dimension in personal growth.

GROWTH CENTERS

In the Big Sur region of California, 150 miles south of San Francisco, set like a jewel beside the sea, is Esalen, the prototype of scores of growth centers in the United States. Michael Murphy, together with his Stanford classmate, Richard Price, founded Esalen Institute in 1962. It was their dream that it should be a center to explore and expand and enhance the human potential. It began as a kind of weekend retreat center to which eminent persons such as Paul Tillich and Abraham Maslow (in the humanistic psychology circle) came to ponder the great issues related to man. In 1956 Michael Murphy traveled to India where he spent eighteen months in a community founded by Sr. Aurobindo, the originator of Integral Yoga. He returned from India with the vision of founding Esalen.

Under the imaginative leadership of the founders, Esalen's program has moved from lectures and discussions to regular week-long study courses and workshops lasting three months

[9] Cf. Claudio Naranjo, "Contributions of Gestalt Therapy," *Ways of Growth*, ed. Herbert A. Otto and John Mann (New York: Viking Press, 1969), pp. 128–46.

or even a year. Since 1960 about 120,000 persons have enrolled in its activities.

Esalen does not have a narrow view of man. It is open to all philosophies and all serious students, though because of Mike Murphy's keen interest in Asian philosophy and Eastern religion it has been especially open to insights and practices of the East. It is a meeting place of scientists concerned about man, how he functions and where he is going. But the leadership of Esalen has studiously avoided allowing any one group to capture the flag and make Esalen into a center committed to a single point of view or a single set of methods. It is a place for turning on without drugs, and for many a sign of hope. Eventually most leaders in the Human Potential Movement show up at Esalen.

The growing public interest in the Human Potential Movement is evidenced by the development of other Growth Centers, built on the style of Esalen, which have sprung up all over the country. The Growth Centers are the Human Potential Movement's first institutions. Now there are at least 100 such centers in the United States. They vary in their program and specialization but usually a great variety of programs are offered: laboratory training: in human relations, psychodrama, dance therapy, art therapy, poetry therapy, Gestalt therapy, sensitivity training, sensory awareness training, encounter, hypnosis, meditation, yoga, group dynamics, transactional analysis, recreation and play therapy.

Herbert A. Otto says:

> The experiences offered at these growth centers are based on several hypotheses:
>
> 1) that the average healthy person functions at a fraction of his capacity;
>
> 2) that man's most exciting life-long adventure is actualizing his potential;
>
> 3) that the group environment is one of the best settings in which to achieve growth; and
>
> 4) that personality growth can be achieved by anyone willing to invest himself in this process.[10]

Growth Centers can be found in almost all major metropolitan areas: Aureon, Anthos, Group Labs, GROW, and many others in New York City; Center for the Study of the Person

---

[10] *Saturday Review*, December 20, 1969, p. 17. Copyright 1969 Saturday Review, Inc.

and Western Behavioral Science Institute in La Jolla, California; Transpersonal Institute in Palo Alto; Laos House in Austin, Texas; Kairos in San Diego; Quest in Washington; Center for the Whole Person in Philadelphia. An extensive list of all Growth Centers can be obtained from the Association of Humanistic Psychology.

In these centers experiencing is offered to individuals but also to special groups: married couples and unmarried couples, divorced people, separated people, old people, drug addicts, ex-drug addicts, teachers, homosexuals, students, clergy, etc. And today most of these places are very busy because the Human Potential Movement, whose outposts they are, is really catching on.

ENCOUNTER GROUPS

Though Growth Centers vary widely in their philosophies, leadership styles and in what they offer, there is one approach which most of them have in common: they all make use of the methodology of encounter.

Encounter groups focus on the individual and help him develop a sense of self-awareness. According to Arthur Burton,

> In encounter groups, there is only the ancient understanding that community, set in a framework of honesty, openness and responsibility, is enlivening and healing. And this "community healing" is vastly different from group therapy or group recreation. Encounter groups are "soul groups," in which the basic parameters of the human condition are opened for all persons to share. There is no agenda. What purpose there is is merely to live more fully and to experience more deeply.[11]

Carl Rogers in his recent book *Carl Rogers on Encounter Groups* summarizes what he judges to be the practical hypotheses which tend to be held in common by all of these groups:

> A facilitator can develop, in a group which meets intensively, a psychological climate of safety in which freedom of expression and reduction of defensiveness gradually occur.
>
> In such a psychological climate many of the immediate feeling reactions of each member toward others, and of each member toward himself, tend to be expressed.

---

[11]Arthur Burton, ed., *Encounter* (San Francisco: Jossey-Bass, 1969), p. 2.

A climate of mutual trust develops out of this mutual freedom to express real feelings, positive and negative. Each member moves toward greater acceptance of his total being—emotional, intellectual, and physical—as it is, including its potential.

With individuals less inhibited by defensive rigidity, the possibility of change in personal attitudes and behavior, in professional methods, in administrative procedures and relationships become less threatening.

With the reduction of defensive rigidity, individuals can hear each other, can learn from each other, to a greater extent.

There is a development of feedback from one person to another, such that each individual learns how he appears to others and what impact he has in interpersonal relationships.

With this greater freedom and improved communication, new ideas, new concepts, new directions emerge. Innovation can become a desirable rather than a threatening possibility.

These learnings in the group experience tend to carry over, temporarily or more permanently, into the relationships with spouse, children, students, subordinates, peers, and even superiors following the group experience. [12]

HOW ARE SHALOM RETREATS RELATED TO THE HUMAN POTENTIAL MOVEMENT: SCIENTIFIC STUDY OF GROUPS, HUMANISTIC PSYCHOLOGY, ENCOUNTER GROUPS AND GROWTH CENTERS?

We are right in the middle of it. We have learned much, have drawn much from and have been powerfully affected by experiences in the Human Potential Movement, at some of its Growth Centers, at the National Training Labs, at Esalen and with Dan Casriel. We have appropriated some of its methods and what we do falls easily under the above description of encounter by Carl Rogers. BUT THERE IS THIS CENTRAL DIFFERENCE: we do our work at a Christian Retreat and Study Center; we are unashamedly Christian in our style of life and leadership as well as in our emphasis on the nature of Christian love. Drawing on the rich resources of the Human Potential Movement we carry out a ministry and conduct research, believing that God is at work in the retreats, and that the rich symbolism of the biblical story and a Christian understanding of the nature of love add a new dimension to the Human Potential Movement now sweeping the country.

---

[12] Rogers, op. cit., p. 6.

CHAPTER 3

The Components of a Shalom Retreat

Imagine us now on our mountain top; a company of eighteen persons, nine men and nine women. We are strangers. We are there for many different reasons. As a group we are alone, separated from the turmoil of a busy world and its demands. Excitement is in the air. Something is about to happen—is happening. The chances are good that strangers will learn to love each other; will assist in each other's growth; will share the depths of fear, anger and pain; will know joy; will reflect and celebrate.

Our Schedule

Thursday Evening		Dinner Community Building
Friday	8 A.M.	Breakfast and Morning Prayer
	9 A.M.	Marathon Begins
Saturday	9 A.M.	Marathon Ends Sleep Begins
	6 P.M.	Dinner
	7 P.M.	Feedback Begins Ends anywhere between 2 A.M. and 4 A.M. on Sunday morning
Sunday	8:30 A.M.	Breakfast
	9:30 A.M.	Theological Reflection Celebration
	12:00 P.M.	Concluding Meal
	1:00 P.M.	The Retreat Is Over

Food is constantly available for any who want it, though three times a day hot food is brought in. Time is taken occasionally as an eating break because oral needs are generally high.

The basic components of a Shalom retreat are: community building, the marathon, feedback, theological reflection and celebration.

I. COMMUNITY BUILDING

Immediately after supper each retreatant takes a place in the mattress circle and community building begins, consisting of the following parts:

A. *Introduction to Kirkridge.* Here we introduce Kirkridge as an experimental institution. Everyone who attends a retreat at Kirkridge is automatically a Kirkridger. We hope that they will grasp the Kirkridge intention of linking strong opposites: social-action and Christian worship; picketers and pray-ers.

B. *How do you feel?* "Tell us your name and in one word how you feel." We do not emphasize last names here and we urge people to keep their profession secret if they feel that such knowledge by the group would in any way put them in a box. Each, of course, does as he chooses, but we do encourage strongly that people get out of their box which others have built for them or which they have built for their own protection. We encourage each to try out new behavior.

To give one's name and tell how he feels, is the first offering which each makes to the community. Some replies relative to feeling come out in many ways: "good," "scared," "exhilarated," "hopeful," "I want to run," etc. This way of asking for feelings provides rapid clues for the leaders relative to what is already going in the group.

C. *How we got into this and what we intend.* In a brief period of time we explain how we got into the Human Potential Movement and what relevance we see it to have for the life of the church. We describe our research and what some of the possible implications are for the life of the church.

We tell candidly about our own experiences in the Human Potential Movement: how they have affected us personally, in our marriage, with our children and in our work. We try to model openness here. As leaders we believe in vulnerability as a style and we do not ask of any others what we are not willing to do ourselves.

D. *We talk about Culture Island.* We are here together. We are alone as a group. We have never been together before and are not likely to be together again as a group. But this is our moment in history together. It is our time. "Try out some new behavior. Take risks for the sake of your own growth." We will share deep feelings and deep confidences.

We then ask the retreatants to enter a covenant binding us not to reveal to others the confidences we will share. We hold that the hours of the retreat are confidential and that they have at least the protection of the office of the pastor, the lawyer, the medical doctor or the counselor. We say, "You can tell your own story but not somebody else's story."

The retreatants then sign a statement to the effect that they will indeed keep confidential all information about other members of the group; that they have their therapist's and physician's permission to participate in the retreat.

E. *Two rules to remember:*

1. No drugs or hard liquor; this includes tranquilizers and pep pills too.

2. We all agree to stay. "Even though you may feel that it is absolutely imperative to leave, we hope you will talk it over with the group first." During our series of retreats only one person has ever left. That was on our first retreat before we made the rule. None has ever discussed with the whole group the possibility of leaving.

F. *The FIRO-B.* As an important part of our research relative to behavior, we give the FIRO-B Test, a test developed by William C. Schutz. FIRO stands for Fundamental Interpersonal Relations Orientation. "It signifies the basic idea that every person orients himself in characteristic ways toward other people and the basic belief that knowledge of these orientations allows for consideration and understanding of individual behavior and the interaction of people."[1]

The test is built upon the foundation that people need people for three kinds of relations: inclusion, control, and affection. Furthermore people need people to receive from and to give to. These are called "wanted behavior" and "expressed behavior."

---

[1]William C. Schutz, *The Interpersonal Underworld* (Palo Alto, Calif.: Science & Behavior Books, 1967), preface.

Schutz says:

> With respect to an interpersonal relation, inclusion is concerned primarily with the formation of a relation, whereas control and affection are concerned with relations already formed. Within existent relations, control is the area concerned with who gives orders and makes decisions for whom, whereas affection is concerned with how emotionally close or distant the relation becomes. Inclusion is concerned with the problem of in or out, control is concerned with top or bottom and affection with close or far.[2]

The test is a measuring instrument developed to assess how people characteristically behave with respect to these needs. The test is given also a minimum of four months after the retreat. Results of these tests relative to our retreatants is reported in chapter 4.

G. *We explain that we will encourage hugging* as an outward sign of giving love to a person. Everyone is free to do as he chooses—to engage in it or not—to act on his or her feelings. He may simply say to another person, "I do not wish to be hugged," thereby also acting out a feeling.

Since hugging may have some erotic or sexual implications, we explain our own marriage covenant—in loving each frees the other to love yet others. But we remind them of much publicity relative to looseness of sexual mores in some encounter groups and that we do not encourage extramarital going to bed. But each person is responsible for his or her own behavior. We do not intend to be their momma and papa. We just want them to know at the beginning where we stand.

H. *The double circle.* In order to participate in the next event the group moves from the mattress circle to another area of the room. Here chairs are arranged in two concentric circles so that the people face each other. We give the following instructions:

> For the next thirty minutes or so we will share feelings with each other. I will give you a series of two-minute discussion subjects. Each time the subject changes, the person who sits in the outside circle will move to his left so that he will have another partner. In this way we will share some of our feelings with at least half of the group. First, tell each other what it is about

---

[2]William C. Schutz, *Joy: Expanding Human Awareness* (New York: Grove Press, 1967), p. 120. Copyright © 1967 by William C. Schutz. Reprinted by permission of Grove Press, Inc.

yourself that you really like, that you feel good about and that you affirm as a positive quality.

The following questions are discussed in like manner, each with a different partner: What do you do when you get angry? What has been your greatest hurt in life? How do you feel about death? How do you react when someone expresses anger toward you? Of what are you most afraid? How do you feel about being alone? Tell a great mountaintop experience of your life. How do you feel when you first come into a group? What do you expect to gain from this weekend?

I. *Seeing and touching.* This is a nonverbal exercise in which each person is asked to encounter every other person present by alternately looking steadily into the other person's eyes and touching his or her head and face. At the end everybody is asked to express whatever feeling surfaces, to hug, shake hands, or simply walk away.

Something of the power of this simple nonverbal method is underscored by Silvan S. Tomkins:

> The significance of the face in interpersonal relations cannot be exaggerated. Not only is it a communication center for the sending and receiving of information of all kinds, but because it is the organ of affect expression and communication, it is also necessarily brought under strict social control. There are universal taboos on looking too directly into the eyes of the other because of the likelihood of affect contagion, as well as escalation; because of the unwillingness to express affect promiscuously; and because of concern lest others achieve control through knowledge of one's otherwise private feelings. Man is primarily a voyeuristic animal, not only because vision is his most informative sense, but also because the shared eye-to-eye interaction is the most intimate relationship possible between human beings.
>
> Only the young or the young in heart are entirely free of the taboo.[3]

Most of the retreatants find this experience a very enlivening one. In the feedback session toward the end of the retreat it is frequently referred to, people remembering how others behaved and what their feelings were about them.

---

[3]From Silvan S. Tomkins in *Challenges of Humanistic Psychology,* ed. James F. Bugental (New York: McGraw-Hill, 1967), p. 57. Copyright 1967 by McGraw-Hill, Inc. Used with permission of McGraw-Hill Book Company.

J. *The love ball.* At the end of the evening we create a very tight circle called a "love ball." When all is very silent and we are much aware of each other's presence, we make the sound "OM," each blending his voice in the way he chooses. After some time we move into the full-orbed sound of "Shalom." When it has reached a crescendo, we are in silence for awhile, then I say: "Look around you. See who is here. They are your people, your family for these days. You are on an important journey together." Then I add, "We encourage you not to stay up and talk, since the marathon will begin tomorrow and you will need your strength."

II. THE MARATHON

The marathon technique, an extended period of accelerated interaction, was first developed by Frederick H. Stoller. With the assistance of George R. Bach, the powerful implications of this technique were opened up and the procedure clarified. Though we have invented our own style we learned a lot from Stoller. In this paragraph he emphasizes the distinctive style of leaders.

> The major practitioners of this approach share most of the basic underlying assumptions. However, there are variations, both in ideas and practice, as well as emphases which are individual. Because of the special importance of personal involvement on the part of the group leader, individual style takes on a heightened significance. The values, personal preferences, and especially the view of life and the world which are part of the group leader's individual system color the proceedings of a marathon group; a marathon experience is qualitatively different because of the presence of a particular group leader.[4]

Some of the Reasons We Use the Marathon Method

1. In a twenty-four-hour period we get in three eight-hour days of continuous accelerated interaction. Time is compressed. Contrariwise, a group meeting only intermittently wastes time in warming up, and group involvement rises and falls.

---

[4]Frederick H. Stoller, *Marathon Group Therapy* (Youth Studies Center School of Public Administration, Von Klein Smid Center for International and Public Affairs, University of Southern California), pp. 2–3.

2. Readiness to be involved is cumulative, especially for some people. One needs to "work" when he is ready. In other types of meetings a person may be ready to "work" just at session-end. The marathon is a pressure cooker providing substantial time for continuous contact and cumulative emotion.

3. It provides gestation-time for the development of intimacy. The world recedes, people become very important to each other.

4. Frequently the critical breakthrough for one person occurs when the group is focusing on someone else.

5. Events have time to occur which never could be planned.

6. There is plenty of time available to work with each person who wants it and there is no easy escape for anyone by way of the clock.

7. For some people, the experiencing of physical tiredness makes it possible for them to be open and honest in a new way.

How the Marathon Is Divided

The marathon period is divided into two parts: the sharing of pilgrimage data and work on the mat.

Pilgrimage data. Each person is allotted seven minutes in which to share what he will with the group. To feed their imagination we pose the following questions:

How do you feel about yourself as a child, adolescent, adult?

How do you feel about yourself now?

What was the quality of relationship between your parents?

What was your relationship to your father, mother, siblings?

How does your life appear now?

Do you have something specific you want to work on during the marathon?

If you are married, how do you feel about your mate?

We find people amazingly candid. Many people who could not imagine talking intimately about themselves for seven minutes, feel they have barely begun when the bell rings.

We believe it is important to begin the marathon in this way. During most of the marathon the emphasis will be on feelings. We tell them, "This is a 'belly trip' as contrasted with a 'head trip.'" There will not be much time during the marathon to go on archeological expeditions that deal mostly with our past. Man is three-dimensional: past, present and future, and it is important that we see each other from all of these perspectives.

This technique also requires everyone to give something of himself to the group; because crucial feelings come tumbling out as people talk about themselves, strong fellow-feelings begin to develop. Often weeping has begun by this time; people weeping for themselves and for each other. Community builds and important identifications and liaisons begin to form.

Work on the mat. "To work" is to be the center of the group's attention. And in our method the "person working" assumes his place in the center on a mattress. We give the following instructions about mat work:

1. We will push you to get involved. But you are in control. As soon as you say "stop," we will stop pushing.
2. Claim the mat whenever you want the help of the group.
3. When you are there, "let go," give up your control, trust the group. Let it all "hang out."
4. Stay with your feelings.
5. No physical violence. This seems to be permissible in some places but not here. On the other hand, you may be as violent or as vile or as picturesque as you wish in your language. Anything goes in the use of language.
6. Don't give advice.
7. Don't ask "why" questions, e.g., why do you feel this way? The important fact is that you *do* feel the way you feel.
8. No subgrouping, i.e., talking with the person next to you while a person is working on the mat. There is no unforgiveable sin in the marathon, but subgrouping is next to it. The person working is entitled to the full attention of the whole group.
9. Anyone is free at any time to get food or go to the toilet, but no more than two are to be gone from the pit at once and they are not to subgroup while they are gone.
10. No one cries alone. Find your best way of being present to and for the weeper.
11. Say what you feel and feel what you say. Be intellectually and emotionally honest.
12. Act yourself into a new way of thinking. You've wasted too much time already trying to think your way into a new way of acting.

The mat work begins. After the pilgrimage data has been

presented, after we have had a noon meal and have all returned to the pit, we remind them that we are primarily now concerned about feelings, fear, anger, and pain as they block the experiencing of love and joy. We are not interested in head trips or archeological expeditions. We explain that the leaders will model the methods and the style of helping the person on the mat and as the group catches on, they are free to help the person in whatever way they can. All can help from the very beginning through empathy and by being there for the other persons. We emphasize that feelings are not moral, they are neither good or bad, they simply are. The marathon process gives our unqualified "Yes" to the question, "Do I have a *right* to my feelings?" Later we also answer the question, "Do I have *responsibility* for my feelings?" Here, too, the answer is a strong affirmative.

Who's got a feeling? That question is asked at the beginning. A silence follows—sometimes short and sometimes long and soon someone is on the mat. It has been our experience in all of our retreats (with the possible exception of one) that as soon as one person is off the mat, another is swiftly there. The scenario varies with each person; for each person it is unique.

When the person lies down on the mat, many gather around and touch him. Vulnerability is here acted out in that the person lies flat on his back. In the long history of religion, the laying on of hands has had an important place. We invoke it here and the person on the mat senses through the hands that he is in the midst of caring community; he is not alone, the people who are there with him really care. We are convinced that this caring, the release of the power to give and receive love occasions the miracles of the retreat.

Each person on the mat during the course of the retreat receives the full attention of the group and we utilize the methods that we think will best help the person get in touch with his deep feelings. Each person receives as much loving attention from the group as he needs and we try never to hurry anyone; but the pressure is always on not playing games, wasting the group's time.

PRIMARY METHODS USED IN SHALOM RETREATS

We do not rely upon a single method but have developed our

own synthesis: The Casriel method, Gestalt methods and encounter, and to these we add a number of subsidiary methods.

The Casriel Method[5]

Daniel Casriel, M.D. who practices in New York City has developed a method of group therapy called AREBA, Accelerated Re-education of Emotions, Behavior and Attitudes. He maintains that living is the pursuit of pleasure and the avoidance of pain. Thus a child decides at an early age whether he will put up with the pain of being frustrated in his needs by those who take care of him or whether he will withdraw from them. Acceptors are those who stay related by accepting the pain while Rejectors decide the pain is intolerable.

Casriel maintains that today many people are out of touch with their feelings. They dare not acknowledge them because they learned at an early age that the expression of feelings is often followed by withholding of love, if not by punishment or derision.

According to Casriel, we make different responses to avoid pain: some of us become fearful, others angry and still others withdraw. In his groups he encourages people to take the risk of expressing what they feel, to express it in as strong a manner as they know how. It is a cathartic experience to get fear, anger, and pain out of your system at last. All of us have been programmed to keep the lid on our feelings to the point where we find people who no longer feel anything at all.

Persons who find it quite easy to express pain—they cry a lot, become depressed—must be helped to surface the anger which lies underneath while persons who became angry and "blow their top" at the slightest provocation have to get in touch with the underlying pain.

Casriel considers a person emotionally healthy who is able to give and receive love but who can also express and receive anger. Most of us learned at an early age that it was dangerous and/or painful to express how we felt. We then became sneaky about it, found seemingly acceptable ways of expressing our

---

[5]See Daniel Casriel, *So Fair a House: The Story of Synanon* (Englewood Cliffs, N.J.: Prentice-Hall, 1964) and Daniel H. Casriel, M.D., and David Deitch, "Time Extended Group Therapy," Jules H. Masserman, ed., *Current Psychiatric Therapies* (New York: Grune & Stratton, 1968).

feelings anyway, though "sideways." The method helps people get their feelings out "straight."

When applying the Casriel method of helping people get in touch with their impacted fear, anger, and pain, we can easily observe how a person becomes frightened of any of these feelings. They have built up over the years to the point where he fears them.

On the whole it is fairly clear that women find it quite easy to get in touch with pain but resist getting hold of their anger. Men, on the other hand, have been conditioned from an early age on to believe that boys and men don't cry, that it is more acceptable to express angry feelings than hurt feelings. However, among Christian people, the feeling is prevalent that it is "nobler" to feel and express pain than to feel and express anger. We find this especially true among the clergy.

In our retreats we attempt to help people become aware of feelings they may not even know exist. And we encourage them to express them at a "gut level," often suggesting a method which will help them to get these feelings out, not just verbally but bodily—pounding, hitting, screaming.

Elisabeth and I studied with Dr. Casriel over a six-months' period of time and participated in his groups and marathons. We are much indebted to him for what we learned about the method and about ourselves. It was our training with him which encouraged us to dig deeper into our own resources in the Christian religion, an understanding which we believe is richer and deeper than the one he utilizes. He believes that "love is an emotion which gives pleasure. It may come and go and come again as any feeling does." As we have indicated in chapter 2, our interpretation is quite different.

The Encounter Method

A sign on the wall says, "Encounter is the owning up to your emotions, no matter how threatening, painful or embarrassing they may be." Though in the marathon the focus stays largely with the individual as he works through some aspect of his feeling world on the mat, we encourage everybody to express toward other persons in the group what they may be feeling toward them. If they feel close to a person, they may wish to go and sit by him or her. If they are angry at them, we encourage them to get it out either by a verbal barrage or by some such device as an Indian wrestling match, where they can test their own strength, deal with the top-dog/under-dog issue, or feelings of losing versus winning. These activities may in turn get them in touch with deep feelings which have nothing to do with the other combatant.

Gestalt Methods

We often use Gestalt methods—methods which were developed by Frederick Perls. He taught an existentialist form of psychiatry with an emphasis on body language, awareness of what a person experiences in the here-and-now. It pays much attention to a person's tone of voice, body gestures, physical mannerisms, etc. When a person is confronted with a conflictual situation, such as "I would like to but I don't dare" or, "I want to but I don't know whether I'll like it" he is encouraged to enact the alternatives and become fully involved in the actual experience of the two alternative possibilities of behaving. By "taking sides," enacting divergent desires or feelings, a person becomes more clearly aware of interior forces in himself which are in opposition to his conscious self-image. Using the Gestalt approach with dreams means enacting the dream in the Now. The dreamer is encouraged to act as if he were the various persons and objects in his dream, i.e., to experience them as forces that are at work within himself which he projected "out there" and which he should reassimilate so that he can be in control of them.

Subsidiary Methodologies

Fantasy. According to Herbert Otto, "development and cultivation of the fantasy stream is a means of helping the imagination to flourish. This can open the door to increased creativity. The willful and conscious development of our capacity to fantasize is a key concept in the actualizing of our human potential."[6] We use the fantasy method as a tool to help people deal with whatever the central question is with which they are struggling. Often we ask the retreatants to share their fantasy with the group and it turns out that all of us enjoy taking this trip into the land of imagination where anything is possible, dreams become true, answers are found

---

[6] Herbert A. Otto, *Group Methods to Actualize Human Potential* (Beverly Hills, Calif.: Holistic Press, 1970), p. 370.

to questions with which a person may have struggled for a long time.

Role-playing. In role-playing a person is asked to enact another significant person, so he speaks and acts as if he were that person, spouse, parent, child, or a person with whom the role-player is in conflict. Hopes, past hurts, and disappointments are portrayed in a more feeling way than if a person simply reports an event of the past with which he could not come to grips. Many times during role-playing a leader or other members of the retreat become an alter ego; i.e., we verbalize those thoughts and feelings which are blocked either because they are considered unpermissible or too dangerous in view of the reaction they might call forth. This device often helps a person come unstuck by getting to the real feeling.

Hold down. Some people feel very much as if they are being manipulated and controlled by others, so they themselves cannot or should not assert themselves. We ask such a person to lie on the mat on his back and others in the group hold down his arms and legs and another person lies across his belly. The person is then urged to get up, to rid himself of those who are limiting his freedom. We find that often a person is really able to get in touch with his deep-seated feelings of anger at other people by this method.

Break-in and break-out. Often there is in the group a person who has very ambivalent feelings about wanting to be included in the group. The group makes a tight circle with arms around each other's shoulders and the person is asked to get into the circle by whatever means he chooses, though not violently. (Violence is forbidden here, also, though the person may talk violently.) By this method some people begin to realize that they really do want to be included and others become quite anxious, and they try obviously very hard either by talk or muscle to break into the circle.

Just the opposite of the previous description is the break-out method. In this instance the tight circle is formed again and a person who feels himself enclosed in a box (role) is encouraged to get out. This, too, often gets a person in touch with deep feelings.

Mattress pound or struggle. One of the important reasons we work on mattresses is that they can be used in many ways. It certainly makes it possible for the person to express his anger physically. We often help people remember how to have a tantrum, screaming and flailing their arms and legs. Sometimes, too, when a person is in touch with deep anger, we simply build a cage of the mattresses and let the person express his full anger without endangering himself or others around him.

Asking for love. We believe it is of great importance to feel and verbalize what we need. All too often a person believes his fellowman is going to be able to guess what his feelings and needs are. In the course of the marathon we frequently point to another sign hanging on the wall, that says: "You cannot love another person, that is, behave toward him so as to foster his happiness and growth unless you know what he needs. And you cannot know what he needs unless he tells you." It makes a difference whether we state that we need to be loved in front of one person at a time and state our need to that person. The fear of rejection which is so great in all of us makes us choose the easier route of simply addressing a whole group with a generalized statement.

Many people, particularly religious types, believe that we cannot receive without first giving or then giving in return. When we ask a person to go around the circle and ask others for a nonverbal expression of love like a hug, we encourage them to keep their arms hanging down alongside their body, i.e., not to hug back but simply to "take in" whatever their friend is trying to communicate by hugging them.

On-the-spot invention. We try to take our clues from a group member in terms of the tool or method which might best help him to deal with an area of his life where he wishes to grow or change. At one retreat we had a woman who was angry report that she had to be "the rock" for everybody around her. She fell easy prey to their dependency needs because "rock" was her self-image. It proved to be very meaningful to her to be able to go outside the lodge at Kirkridge and with a sledge hammer smash a big rock to pieces, thus symbolizing that she was a feeling person who had needs of her own and wanted her friends to meet them. By smashing the rock she smashed, too, the image which she abhorred.

One couple described their relationship in such a way that it was clear to the group that the wife had placed her husband on a pedestal. We asked him to stand on a chair and talk to his wife. When this couple began to converse it was clear that the husband did not want to be on that pedestal at all. We then had them reverse their roles and she spoke down to him. This enactment helped her focus on some of her feelings regarding the top-dog/bottom-dog roles she found her husband and herself stuck in.

The head-and-leg lift. This is a nonverbal method which is enjoyed very much since it helps us get in touch with a different set of bodily sensations and also enables us to receive from others. This method is carried out in groups of three people who are compatible and already have good feelings toward each other. One of the persons lies flat on his back, closes his eyes, and relaxes. The other two people kneel by his side for a moment or two in a contemplative, thankful, and good-will attitude toward their friend. Then they take their positions at the head and feet of the person. First, the person's head is slowly lifted from the floor, then turned to the right, then to the left, very slowly and then put back on the floor. Next, his legs are raised, again very slowly and fairly high and then lowered back on the floor. The persons then change positions and lift the head and the legs simultaneously, very slowly until they reach the comfortably high position at the same time; they begin to lower head and legs until they reach the floor at the same time. Each person of the threesome has his turn.

Rock and roll. After a person has worked on the mat we "rock and roll" him as a way of expressing the group's love toward him. First, he is asked to stand in the middle of a circle formed by about six–eight people. He is asked to close his eyes, and trust himself to the will and love of the group as they pass him around several times. They then lift him up and, holding him at about shoulder height, the group lovingly and tenderly rocks him back and forth for quite some time. This is done in total silence. He is then gently put down on the floor and those who wish go and hug him while he continues to lie on the floor. Usually the whole group participates. It is a mini-celebration, a ritual with much meaning. This will be discussed in more detail in the chapter on celebration.

And then it is over. The marathon ends on time—usually at 9:00 on Saturday morning. In all our experiencing we have seldom had a person go to sleep. When a person nods he is dutifully awakened by one of his fellows.

Now the dawn has come. Many people are amazed how

quickly the twenty-four hours have sped. Most have lost consciousness of how long they have been together. Now we urge them strongly to go to sleep. "Don't stay up and talk even though you may feel quite turned on. There is much yet to do in the retreat and you will need your strength."

After a quick breakfast, almost everyone wants to get to bed. Many sleep for eight full hours; some are not quite able to make it and are roaming around after six hours of sleep. For them there is food available and great beauty. It is 9 A.M. Saturday. The marathon is over.

III. FEEDBACK

After a good sleep and a delicious dinner, the group assembles again in the pit for feedback. It is now around 7 P.M., Saturday.

The purpose of feedback is to provide a stated time and opportunity in which each person in the retreat gives data to every other person on how he appears to others and how he has related to the whole group. Of course, feedback has been going on constantly in the course of the retreat but this is a stated time in which the whole group participates while feedback is given to a single person.

Feedback does not always start on time since some people may want to work on the mat. In this case priority is given to that working and the feedback is delayed.

The rules of feedback on a Shalom Retreat are as follows:

1. Each person in the group receives feedback from everyone else.
2. The person receiving the feedback cannot respond until he has received feedback from everyone.
3. The spouse is the last to give feedback.

Benefits for the Receiver:

1. He learns about himself. This is one of the reasons he came to the retreat.
2. Usually a person's self-image is strengthened; he is perceived by his peers as lovable, beautiful, strong, good, tender, whatever.
3. He may see his problem or weakness in a new way because of the impact of massed data coming from members of the group.

4. Many times the individual receives much more positive feedback than negative, though he may learn more from the negative.

5. By now a powerful feeling of love has emerged in the retreat and even when the feedback is negative, it is received and listened to with care.

We emphasize that *feedback can be wrong.* It is up to the receiver to make of the feedback what he will. But we do tell this parable. If one person thinks you are a horse, you may receive it as interesting information but not necessarily as more. If two people think you are a horse, it should at least make you thoughtful; if three, it should produce some anxiety; if four, go buy yourself a saddle.

Most people during the feedback are very moved by what they now hear from their friends, are hard-pressed for comments, and often receive them with tears. It is probably true that most people take their feedback very seriously and that they "chew" on it long after the retreat is over.

Benefits for the sender. Since Frederick Stoller has written very meaningfully about this and since our experience is much in line with his interpretation we use his words here:

> Putting aside the benefits to the recipients of feedback for the moment, it places obligations and considerable opportunities for learning upon the sender. These can be categorized as follows: (a) the giver of feedback becomes more in touch with his own fleeting responses which, under ordinary social conventions, become discarded because they are rarely verbalized; (b) it is the obligation of the giver of feedback to specify, as clearly as he can, the basis of his reactions so that he must scan out his own inner state and perceptions more thoroughly than is generally the case; the consequences are that he sets into motion ways of encountering himself more fully; (c) through the range of observations (and lack of observation) the group member makes himself known to the rest of the group in terms of how he perceives the world; his capacity for honesty or deviousness, and how he offers help: in short, the group learns about him through his behavior rather than through the version of himself he would like the group to buy.[7]

Uniqueness of Shalom feedback. 1. For us this is often a very celebrative time. There is generally a great deal of easy

---

[7]Arthur Burton, ed., *Encounter* (San Francisco: Jossey-Bass, 1969), pp. 89–90.

laughter and use of the group's own symbolism and "house jokes." In some deep sense each person receiving feedback is celebrated by the whole group.

2. Sometimes a person who has not emerged at all really comes into focus in the course of his giving feedback. He then reveals himself as having really been present all along.

IV. THE FINAL MORNING

By Sunday morning, though all have worked exceedingly hard, the spirits of most people are usually high. There is a full-orbed sense of intimacy and caring all around; even people who were shy about hugging now express their love in this way. During our entire retreat series we have had only two people who resisted hugging all the way.

After breakfast we are in the pit again. We begin by asking, "How do you feel—in one word?" Most feelings are now on the positive side: "accepted," "warm," "great," "bubbly," "alive."

Theological Reflections

Now we explain to the group that we want their help. A new age has been born, all institutions are in some sense dysfunctional with the culture and have to run to catch up. The church has a lot of running to do. Her style certainly has to be updated but another task that needs doing is the translation of her message into modern idiom. In each new age the task of theology is to retranslate the message in terms of that age. Now we are at the beginning of a new epoch and the changes are so radical that we cannot simply depend upon past-oriented theologians to rearrange theological concepts. A fresh witness needs to be made and a new word spoken by "ordinary" people in the midst of fresh experiencing, putting their meaning down as theological reflections. So we ask all to help by doing some stream-of-consciousness writing in the midst of the retreat experience. If a person is not a Christian, we ask him to write from the perspective of his own religious tradition; if he is not "religious" at all, we ask him to do meaning reflection. We ask them not to worry much about style.

The questions we provide are:

1. What new light does this experience shed upon any of the following:

your understanding of Christianity?
your faith?
the biblical story?

2. Do you see any implications for the local church? For example, do you think the methods used at this retreat are applicable there?

Please write freely and spontaneously out of your feelings and perceptions. Do not try to be precise. If you can, do a stream-of-consciousness kind of writing.

An analysis of all the reflections is in chapters 6 and 7. Here we have a gold mine of material which cannot be exhausted in the reporting in this book. Hopefully others will want to research it. There is no doubt that the methods used in the retreat produce peak experiences for most people. The reflections come to us in the heat of such an experience and therefore the material is very significant.

Celebration

While the retreatants are doing their theological reflections, we make arrangements for the celebration. The place of meeting now becomes the place of special celebration.

The mat has now become an "altar" and our pit the "place of meeting"—crucial biblical terms. A flat, square board is put on the two mattresses and on the board a jug of wine and a loaf of bread. (For those who do not drink wine, a pitcher of grape juice is provided.) We bring out some Bibles, song books—old and new.

When all have gathered again we say, "We have had a beautiful time together. We have met. It is time now to celebrate." To this invitation we add only this: real celebration should rise from common experiencing; unplanned things should happen, and everyone should have a chance to offer something or help determine what the group does.

Then the celebration begins. Each time it is different. Each time it is beautiful. Sometimes very quiet—sometimes noisy. Sometimes both quiet and noisy. Sometimes very individualistic—two by two—celebrating their truth. Sometimes very groupy.

The celebration flows into the concluding meal and the

ending of the retreat. A special analysis of the celebration is found in chapter 8.

The Retreat Is Over

We have seen some people change before our eyes—change in facial expression, vocabulary, gestures, and postures.

For some it has meant a new grasping of their personhood, manhood, womanhood.

For some it has meant a strong movement toward greater authenticity and fulfillment.

Some, not having cried since they were small children, have gotten in touch with a side of their personality long ignored.

Some have wept over a long-ago grief, and some over a recent grief.

All of us have gotten to know ourselves better.

Some have learned to love themselves.

Some have learned to express tenderness and real caring for others.

Now some are more prepared to face the real tasks of the real life they must live.

Some have made a growth choice instead of a fear choice.

Some have identified defenses they now say they intend to give up.

From now on we will all be enabled to love in a warmer and more open fashion. In some sense a healing process has begun by the cathartic emotional experience. Real intimacy has emerged and genuine friendship—some of which will continue in the future.

Many have found that intimate involvement with others and mutual concern can be a source of great joy.

When They Leave

All get the names and addresses and phone numbers of all retreatants. We give out a bibliography and mimeograph sheets with the quotes from the walls. We want to stay in touch with them. We will mimeograph the theological reflections and send them out soon.

As our last act as a group we make a love ball again, the sound of "OM" and "Shalom" blending in beautiful harmony. Then we say, "Remember the first night when we were strangers? Now we are strangers no more. We have met; we have each been strengthened by the love of the other. Shalom!"

CHAPTER 4

The Follow-up Study

INTRODUCTION

We had led several Shalom Retreats before we approached Kirkridge with our research proposal. Many of our former retreatants had reported mountaintop experiences. But we were well aware that glowing reports are not sufficient to influence policy. We knew, too, that a report of a "religious experience," while listened to politely, is not expected to have significant implications relative to a person's behavior. Also we were much aware of articles in popular magazines and journals pointing to lack of research relative to Human Potential methods. We knew that there was practically no research done by the religious community in this area. So we set out to conduct research, to follow our retreatants, to find what effects the experience of the retreat had upon their attitudes, feelings, and behavior and their perspectives on church and world; we wanted to learn if the retreat experience had helped them become more loving persons.

This chapter and the next contain the results of this research. There is good news in these chapters for those who are already interested in the relationship of the Human Potential field and the church. Hopefully the data will encourage others to begin to look with hope toward an alliance between this important movement and the church.

THE RESEARCH DESIGN

We used the same methods at all retreats. The basic principles described in chapter 1 and the components of the retreat described in chapter 3 were held the same. Only the people who came to the retreats were different.

On the following pages we will describe the three groups of retreatants used in this study, the instruments with which we obtained the data on which our findings are based, the evaluative procedures followed, and the findings relative to our first hypothesis.

The Groups Under Study

The core-group, referred to later as *Kirkridge Group*, is made up of participants in Shalom Retreats at Kirkridge. A second group, the *Albright Group*, though it attended a regular retreat at Kirkridge, is being used for comparison; we decided to consider it a separate group because of its homogeneity. All members of this group came from the same college, were single, and on the average twenty years old. Though they did not have to participate in the retreat, they were quite clearly expected to do so since they had chosen "Personality and Theology" as a one-month interim semester course at their college. The third group, the *LaForet Group*, consisted of pastors and their wives who had participated in an eleven-day training conference at LaForet, a United Church conference grounds in Colorado, in the summer of 1969. The conference design included the utilization of Human Potential methods and sociodrama. Since a year and a half had passed since that conference we were very interested to find out what the questionnaires of those pastors and wives would reveal about possible long-range effects of the LaForet experience on their present relationships, their pastoral ministry, and their attitudes and feelings.

The Research Instruments

We used three instruments: a questionnaire, a confidential evaluation, and the FIRO-B test.

A first version of the questionnaire was tried out with the Albright Group. It was then revised: some questions were made more explicit and others were added or deleted. For this reason not all answers of the Albright Group could be compared to those of the Kirkridge and LaForet Groups.

The questionnaire consists of four parts. The first deals with personal data such as age, marital status, profession, previous sensitivity training and a question indicating whether a person had attended the retreat alone, with a friend or his/her spouse. The second part contains questions pertaining to behavior changes; the third provides us with information regarding church membership, denominational affiliation, position in the church, attitudes of pastors and laymen toward each other, experimentation with new forms of worship (celebration) and participation in encounter-type groups, in or outside the local church. Part four gives an account of retreatants' involvement in long-term counseling.

We decided to use a *confidential evaluation* by a "significant other" who had known the retreatant for some time because there is research proving that the effectiveness of sensitivity-training cannot be judged solely by those who participated in such an experience.

As mentioned in chapter 1, we used the *FIRO-B test* at the very beginning of the retreat. Another copy of the same test was sent to retreatants with the rest of the follow-up material (questionnaire and confidential evaluation). We could not use this test for the LaForet Group because we had not asked those people to keep the scores of the FIRO-B test which they had taken at the beginning of that conference in Colorado.

The Collecting of Data

A copy of the letter which accompanied the follow-up material, a sample of both questionnaire and confidential evaluation form are in Appendix A.

For the Albright Group the time span between retreat and follow-up study was four months; for the LaForet Group eighteen months. For the 115 persons among the Kirkridge retreatants to whom follow-up material was sent, the average time span was six months; it was never less than four months. (For details see Table A1 in Appendix B.) We did not include those persons in our study who had attended the last three of the series of twelve Shalom Retreats at Kirkridge because not enough time had passed between their retreat and the time when we began to gather the data. However, some of their theological reflections are included in other chapters.

We sent a reminder to those persons who had not returned questionnaire and FIRO-B test within a month after they had been mailed to them. Of the Kirkridge Group 91 percent (105 persons) sent back that material. For the LaForet Group the figures were 89 percent (31 persons); for the Albright Group 82 percent (14 persons). (See Table A2.)

The data contained in questionnaires, FIRO-B tests, and confidential evaluations were coded for computer processing. The major findings reported here are based on frequency and cross-tabulations.

SUMMARY OF FINDINGS

Instead of offering table after table of numbers and percentages regarding each segment of this study, we decided to put most of them in the appendix. Apart from those tables which give information regarding basic personal data of the retreatants, only those findings will be presented in tabular form that are the most important. All tables showing the prefix A are in Appendix B.

Basic Data

It needs to be pointed out once more that the following findings pertain only to those retreatants who returned the follow-up material. First, we will give an overview of personal data regarding the respondents. (For the sake of clarity this is done in abbreviated form by leaving out decimal points in percentage figures. For details see appendix.)

Age

	Kirkridge	LaForet	Albright
Age range	20–66	28–57	19–22
Average age	40.1	34.8	20
Number respondents	105	31	14

Sex

	Kirkridge	LaForet	Albright
Men	48%	71%	43%
Women	52%	29%	57%

At Kirkridge we try to have as balanced a group as possible

Marital Status

	Kirkridge	LaForet	Albright
Married	87%	100%	—
Single	7%	—	100%
Separated Divorced Widowed	6%	—	—

Geographical Distribution

	Kirkridge	LaForet	Albright*
New York	34%	7%	
Pennsylvania	15%		100%
Metropolitan Washington	14%		
South & Southwest	9%	7%	
New England	9%	7%	
New Jersey	8%		
Midwest	6%	68%	
Canada	6%		
West & Northwest		13%	

*We consider the college their place of residence

Profession

Here we deal only with the Kirkridge Group in detail as the LaForet Group was attended only by pastors and their wives; the Albright Group consisted entirely of students.

Men

21 pastors (42%)
5 executives
(2 in church agencies, 1 in marketing, 1 in advertising, 1 in engineering)
1 manager (research & development)
3 engineers
9 educators
(3 administrators, 3 college teachers, 3 in management-development)
1 guidance counselor
1 psychiatrist
1 dentist
2 psychologists (research)
1 commercial artist
1 planner
1 furniture designer/craftsman
1 telephone installer
1 medical student
1 without profession

Women

23 full-time housewives*
5 teachers
1 school administrator
1 college department chairman
1 guidance counselor
1 social worker
1 mental health counselor
1 adult group worker
1 student activities coordinator
1 physician
5 nurses
1 businesswoman
2 administrative assistants
4 secretaries
1 systems programmer
1 librarian
1 horticulturist
4 students (3 of them older women)

*50% of the married women listed their professional work which means that this high percentage of married women pursues a career besides being housewives.

With Whom Did They Come to the Retreat?

	Kirkridge	LaForet	Albright
With spouse	69%	52%	
Alone	15%	48%	
With friend	16%		100%

7% of the married men and 10% of the married women came to the retreat without spouse (K-group)
The Kirkridge distribution is of course influenced by the fact that we had included a statement in our brochure to the effect that we strongly discouraged people from coming to the retreat alone.

Previous Sensitivity Training

Kirkridge	LaForet	Albright
55%	52%	14%

Long-term Counseling

	Kirkridge	LaForet	Albright
During 5 years preceding retreat	29%	13%	none
At time of retreat	15%	3%	none
Started since retreat	3%	none	none
Terminated since retreat	5%	none	none

Church Membership

Kirkridge	Albright
92%	64%

Denominational Affiliation

All participants in the LaForet Conference were members of the United Church of Christ. We do not know to what churches the Albright students belong.

Kirkridge Group

United Church of Christ	37%	Reformed	2%
Presbyterian	20%	Friends' Meeting	2%
Baptist	10%	Unitarian	2%
Methodist	6%	Lutheran	1%
United Church of Canada	6%	Mennonite	1%
Episcopal	3%	Unknown	3%
Church of the Saviour Washington, D.C.	3%		

Position in Church

	Kirkridge	LaForet	
Layman	30%	7%	(executives' wives)
Clergy	22%	65%	
Clergy wife	16%	22%	
Church executive	3%	7%	
Officer (trustee, deacon, S.S. teacher)	30%		

Behavior Change

Hypothesis: *By blending the Christian concept of the nature of love and Human Potential methods we can initiate significant behavior changes in our retreatants.*

Behavior change as reported on questionnaire. In this section we will quote some of the questions as they had been found in the questionnaire before giving statistical figures and summarizing the findings pertaining to that particular question. The retreatants were encouraged to describe how they perceived changes in their feelings, attitudes, or behavior. Many took advantage of this opportunity and wrote at length about the new behavior that they had observed. We will make ample use of such statements by respondents since they illustrate more vividly than percentage points what some of the effects were which respondents attributed to their retreat experience.

Question: In which of the following areas do you express your needs or your feelings more than you did before the Shalom Retreat? __Need to be loved; __love for others; __anger; __pain; __fear; __joy; __other (please explain); __none of the above.

The table below shows *a high percentage of respondents reported a change in their expression of feelings and needs. This finding is of great significance in view of the frequently reported criticism that sensitivity-training, encounter, and other similar experiences where Human Potential methods are used, lead only to very temporary shifts in feelings and attitudes rather than to lasting changes in behavior.*

Change in Expression of Feelings and Needs

	Kirkridge		LaForet		Albright	
	%	No.	%	No.	%	No.
Need for love	74.3	78	64.5	20	84.6	11
Love for others	79	83	74.0	23	not asked	
Anger	55.2	58	83.9	26	64.3	9
Pain	35.2	37	41.9	13	35.7	5
Fear	23.8	25	38.7	12	28.6	4
Joy	54.3	57	58.1	18	78.6	11
Other	6.7	7	16.7	5	not asked	
None	3.8	4	—	—	not asked	

Those who had checked the category "other," gave the following descriptions: "I am becoming a me"; "trust—it's becoming increasingly possible (safe?) to try to be different. I take more chances with people, and experiment with behaviors that just aren't (weren't?) 'me'"; "expressing feelings more spontaneously and trusting urge to reach out to people more"; "generally being able to relate better and be much more open about myself to others." Two persons mentioned, "physical contact with others and sexuality"; others, "love of self," "guilt," "forgiveness."

Four persons among the Kirkridgers had checked "none of the above." We took a close look at their questionnaires. One showed a big question mark alongside that list of feelings. The way in which this respondent had filled out the rest of the questionnaire indicated that he felt the retreat had helped him become more open and more accepting of other people. Another person among the four discussed here, commented at the end of the questionnaire: "I'm sorry I can't report more results from the Shalom Retreat. This was my fourth encounter. The first one was in May and I feel that it was the most effective for me, probably because it was a brand new experience." Finally, the two persons who had answered almost all questions of the questionnaire to the negative were a couple who had been very disappointed by the retreat experience and upset by the fact that it had in no way met their expectations for spiritual renewal.

It was startling to find that a markedly higher percentage of persons in the LaForet Group than the Kirkridge Group had checked "anger." We proceeded to combine these two groups and analyzed the data for clergy and laity separately. It turned out that 76 percent of the pastors versus 56 percent of the laymen thought they had become more expressive of their anger as a result of the retreat experience (Table A13).

Another revealing difference between pastors and laymen emerged when we compared the figures for the category "need for love." In this instance we focused our attention on pastors and men of other professions. 95 percent of the clergy indicated they were more expressive of their need to be loved than they had been prior to the retreat as compared to 67 percent of men of other professions (Table A14).

We were well aware of the fact that the emphasis at our retreats was heavily on love. In order to find out whether most respondents thought they had become more expressive only of positive feelings, i.e., their need for love, love for others, joy, we grouped all six feelings on that list (see page 74) into three categories. It was encouraging for us to see that 65% of the Kirkridge Group, 84% of the LaForet Group, and 71% of the Albright students had indicated that they considered themselves more expressive of both positive **and** negative feelings as a result of their retreat experience. The distribution for only positive feeling was Kirkridge, 26%; LaForet, 10%; Albright, 14%: for only negative feelings, Kirkridge, 6%; LaForet, 7%; Albright, 14%. The first category contained all responses where any combination and number of positive **and** negative feelings had been checked; the second and third categories were made up of those responses that had one, two, or all three of either the positive or negative feelings checked (Table A15).

The data described earlier regarding the change in pastors' expression of anger explains again why the LaForet Group showed a higher percentage of responses falling into the positive **and** negative categories than was the case for the Kirkridge Group.

Question: Immediately after the Shalom Retreat, did you notice a change in your feelings toward yourself? __Yes __No (Please describe.)

More than 90 percent of the respondents in each of the three groups reported a change in their feelings toward themselves immediately after their retreat experience (Table A16).

Here now are statements made by respondents to describe the change which they had observed in their feelings toward themselves.

> "I experienced a wholeness—a feeling of being 'all together' for maybe the first time in my life."
> "A lot of fear was gone, fear of being inadequate, of not being enough."
> "I felt freer to love and express my love for others without minding any fear of being rejected by others."
> "Encounters such as Kirkridge help me open up, to feel more, risk more—to dare to be vulnerable—to give to people and to receive from them—to be more ME."
> "I felt strongly at peace with myself. The 'do good' toward others was no more necessary."

Several respondents gave particular mention to *a different way of handling their angry feelings.*

> "We have more arguments, but the old hostile impasse is gone and there is no more sniping, cutting and ego-chopping."
> "Arguments and feelings of anger don't last very long now. Amazing! Able to make love after a fight—something which I needed days or weeks to overcome before."
> "Being helped to express my anger, specifically, more openly put my relationship to my wife and our daughters on a more honest and therefore firmer base so that now we can get to the heart of our differences sooner."

Two women mentioned that *tension* which had often bothered them considerably prior to the retreat, was no longer a problem for them. They wrote:

> "I did not know how much I hated myself and was able to be aware of the tenseness in my body—to experience myself when the hate and tenseness was gone, was a new sensation—relaxation and peace."
> "I was experiencing a great deal of 'anxiety' due to my hangups before the retreat. Since then my 'tension headaches' have practically disappeared, a good example of how one's mental state of mind can affect one physically."

Question: Immediately after the Shalom Retreat, did you notice a change in your feelings toward significant others (e.g., your spouse, your children, close friends)? Yes__No__(Please describe.)

Here again the percentage of those respondents in each group who felt their *attitude and feelings toward persons close to them had changed, was higher than 90 percent* (Table A17).

> "I was opened to see people close to me as they were—people like me struggling and yearning for the same thing—love."
> "I felt much closer to the children who were quite surprised and responded in love and a real drop in temper-tantrums. My wife and I found a new relationship of real deep love and concern."
> "I now 'see' him not as the idol of my dreams but as a human with needs, a person with his own feelings and realizing that he had a right to these feelings and ideas. It didn't mean I had to agree or accept them as my own. But I did have to respect them because they are part of him."

Question: Immediately after the Shalom Retreat, did you notice a change in your feelings toward other people (e.g., colleagues at work, friends, neighbors)? Yes__No__(Please describe.)

Around 90 percent of the Kirkridge as well as the LaForet respondents thought there had been a *change in their feelings toward other people* (Table A18). The Albright Group could not be included in this tabulation as our pilot questionnaire did not show this specific question.

> "I just love people more and express it more willingly—without censoring or calculation."
> "Better understanding of how my associates (fellow workers and employees) must feel . . . greater sense of empathy and more concern for them as fellow human beings."
> "The retreat helped me to feel closer to people—to enter into their lives on a more basic level. I don't know how I've done it—but more people come to me with whatever is bothering them. They let me in more often than previous to the retreat" (pastor's wife).

We did expect a large percentage of retreatants to report that they had felt more positively about themselves right after the retreat. Toward the end of each retreat we could easily notice that many persons felt quite elated and positive about themselves. Would these feelings last? Or would the humdrum of everyday living destroy what many persons had learned about themselves and others during the retreat?

The next set of questions on the questionnaire dealt with this concern of ours. We asked whether the respondents had *continued to feel differently* toward themselves, significant others and other people. As the table below shows the percentages of those who felt the change in feelings and attitudes had indeed lasted is very high for the Kirkridge and LaForet Groups. (The Albright Group could not be included because the question regarding continued change had been phrased quite differently.)

Immediate Versus Continued Change in Feelings

	Toward Self				Toward Significant Others				Toward Others			
	Kirkridge		LaForet		Kirkridge		LaForet		Kirkridge		LaForet	
	%	No.	%	No.	%	No.	%	No.	%	No.	%	No.
Immediate change	91.4	96	96.8	30	92.4	97	96.8	30	89.5	94	93.5	29
Continued change	83.3	85	96.8	30	86.3	88	93.5	29	79.6	82	93.5	29

What a surprise to see that more people in the LaForet Group than the Kirkridge Group felt the change in feelings had lasted! This result could not have been expected as the Shalom experience lay eighteen months in the past for the LaForet Group as compared with the four to ten months that had gone by between retreat and follow-up study for the participants in the Kirkridge retreats.

Several respondents commented that similar, reinforcing experiences had been essential for them to continue to grow.

> "Although the change I feel in myself has been more subtle than radical, it is a very real change. The retreat, along with several other reinforcing experiences, has opened me up to myself. Much growing remains to be done . . . and I'm looking forward to it."
>
> "The Shalom Retreat has been a life-changing experience for me and has really started me out on a new track. I don't know where it will lead me but I am glad to be on the way."
>
> "Change for me started very noticeably three years ago and the retreat strengthened and brought about changes faster."

Some comments made at the end of questionnaires revealed that the going had been rough for some retreatants upon their return home.

> "The door opened for a while but the draft was too much for my wife."
>
> "At the close of the retreat I allowed myself to cast out fear and to be raised up through the faith, love, and honesty of the others there. For two or three weeks thereafter I soared to heights of joy I have never known. Then the magic wore off. The tensions of everyday living began to once more undermine me and the fears came back. I mentioned to A. (another retreatant) that I was sorry I had ever gone to the retreat because it lifted me so high it only gave me further to fall. Her reply was, 'I'm glad I went for the same reason. Now, regardless of how far I fall I know that the heights exist and I'll keep trying.' Bless her, she was *so right!*"
>
> "It didn't last—I hurt more now than I did before—either I'm not trying hard enough to communicate or my husband isn't listening."

We knew that those closest to a retreatant, for married people the spouse, were of crucial importance if the retreat experience were to have a lasting effect and result in behavior change. The following at least partly sad account lends support to our decision not to accept married people at our retreats any longer who cannot come to such an event as a couple (except in extraordinary circumstances).

> "The retreat really did something for me and for which I thank you. My wife was leery about my free expression of feelings. She still says I can never go to such a place again, tries to tell me I should not answer the questionnaire . . . and I have not gotten her to fill the other one out honestly and send it. (I am glad you are not accepting men without their spouses anymore.) Still, tho, for the retreat days and the days that followed and my own inner feelings, I thank you."

Behavior change as reported in confidential evaluation. Does the subjective assessment of behavior change correspond with the evaluation made by an outsider, i.e., a person who knows the retreatant well? We were not willing to base our research solely on what retreat-participants had to say about the effect on feelings, attitudes, and behavior which they attributed to their Shalom experience. For this reason we sent a different questionnaire to them with the instructions to give it to a person who knew them well. (See appendix for a sample copy.)

We received 94% of the confidential evaluations about Kirkridge retreatants, 71% about LaForet participants, and 71% about Albright students (Table A19).

It seemed of interest to us to know what the relationship was between the person who had filled out the confidential evaluation and the retreatant who had given him/her that questionnaire. For the Kirkridge Group 66% of the evaluations had been filled out by the spouse of the retreatant, 27% by a friend, 7% by a relative. Laforet: 73% by spouse, 27% by friend. Albright: 100% by friends (Table A20).

The evaluators were first asked to answer the question: "Do you think the behavior of ______ was affected significantly as a result of his/her experience at a Shalom Retreat?"

According to the judgment of a significant other, 89% of the Kirkridge respondents, 95% of the LaForet participants, and 80% of the Albright students included in this study had changed significantly in their behavior (Table A21).

What was the nature of this change in behavior? What aspect of a retreatant's behavior had been most affected by the retreat experience? In order to obtain this information we asked the evaluators: "Please describe the changed behavior as you perceive it."

A content analysis shows that for all three groups the highest percentage of comments deals with the retreatants' *changed self-image*. This is the area where—as described on page 78 (see also Table A16)—the respondents themselves had felt a very noticeable change in their feelings. The following paragraphs will deal with comments related to each of the three categories of behavior change which were most often described by the evaluators and which are represented numerically in the following table.

Content Analysis of Confidential Evaluations

Change in Feelings	Kirkridge		LaForet		Albright	
	%	No.	%	No.	%	No.
Toward self	77.5	69	80.9	17	62.5	5
Toward others	25.8	23	19.1	4	—	—
Handling of anger (conflict management)	48.3	43	57.1	12	37.5	3

Comments made by significant other persons about the *changed self-image* observed in retreatant:

> "He is now more confident about himself and his ability."
> "A new appreciation of her own feelings and a new sexual release and freedom occurred after the experience with a definite and new confidence in her own womanhood."
> "The retreat surfaced a lot of her pain. Under that is a lot of love and a lot of woman. She has been a joy to love and really turned on toward others and me. She got rid of a lot of her not okness and it is great living with an ok woman."

Comments about *changed behavior toward others,* as reported in confidential evaluations:

> "In our relationship he lets me know what is going on with him more. He used to not reveal how he was feeling without much effort on my part. He would also withdraw or withhold love."
> "More able to share his hurts and disappointments. It does not seem nearly so difficult for him to say he is 'wrong'—more willing to let me and others have feelings and to express them without defensive response. He is consciously trying out new behavior that is considerate of others."
> "Rev. X. was so preoccupied before that he did not seem to be conscious of what was going on about him at times. He seemed very troubled. At present he is himself, has so much love and concern for others it is overflowing" (a parishioner about pastor).
> "People see him as one who is sensitive to their needs and is himself needy of their interest and love."

Comments about *change in handling of anger,* as reported in confidential evaluations:

> "There is an increased ability to 'stay in communication' when feelings arise. She used to just 'dig a hole.'"
> "She is more aware of her feelings of pain and anger and is more able to express and share them with others."
> "I observe a new ability to express her negative feelings about me and my actions to me directly instead of internalizing as she did previously or coming at me sideways."
> "I think he can deal with conflict so much better—before he would unconsciously or consciously turn away from it—sometimes he would actually become immobilized. The other night in a group situation we had an emotionally-charged episode building up—and it had to be dealt with and he became the confronter in the most natural way—and he stayed in there and pushed and believe me, it was and is something to celebrate" (pastor's wife about her husband)!

Several comments dealt with the *effect the retreat had had on a marital relationship:*

> "I know that this experience—plus numerous others—have made this a different couple even from the people they were when they came to Kirkridge."
> "Most obvious to me was her new commitment to the task of 'working' on our relationship, a renewed intention to love—in fact, a new understanding of love as an act of the will, rather than an automatic emotion. Behaviorally, this has produced a 'stick-to-it-iveness'; a pattern of 'hanging in there' and working it through when communication crises arise between us, rather than withdrawing into silent noncommunication, as both of us have done in the past."
> "His new awareness of the world of feelings since the retreat has made a big difference in our marriage."

Among the quotes in the previous section of this chapter were two by women who had reported that tenseness and tension-headaches had markedly decreased in frequency, if not totally disappeared. What a surprise then to find a confidential evaluation which dealt with the same issue. A fiancee wrote:

> Before the retreat she had frequent and serious headaches which were caused by her suppression of feelings, mainly of her experiences in Africa but also personal anxiety about acceptance and mate selection; and as a result of the retreat she is now in contact with her feelings and as she deals with them she no longer has the headaches.

Some evaluations stated quite clearly that a retreatant had felt as if on a mountaintop upon his/her return from the retreat but that these *feelings had not lasted.* A pastor wrote:

> The observable change was temporary but marked enthusiasm, a "high" which was soon undercut by pressures at home. I believe the more lasting change is a renewed hunger for a fuller life and I'm sure the Shalom Retreat is one of the reasons she stayed in a Come-Alive-Group in our congregation.

Among the confidential evaluations were some that dealt with the *influence that other or similar experiences* had had on a retreatant just as we had found such statements in the questionnaires.

> "She was willing to enter into other encounters which helped. It was good for her therapy. It would have been far less significant if she had not been in psychotherapy at the time."

> "It's difficult to isolate the effects of this particular experience for as you probably know she's been into several related things lately. The most striking factor I think was due to the retreat being explicitly Christian—its positive influence was in the context of much less risk and anxiety—I think it moved her another step along the way in self-confidence—freedom to risk."

We now need to look at those confidential evaluations which stated that *no change in behavior* had occurred as a result of the Shalom Retreat experience.

Two evaluators felt they were not really qualified to make an evaluation. One of them was a parishioner who wrote he had known his pastor well only since he had been to the retreat; the other was from the daughter of a retreatant who stated that her contacts with her mother were infrequent and that behavior changes in her mother might for that reason escape her notice.

Three persons who evaluated their spouses' behavior as not changed, wrote:

> "He is on a growing edge, better understands his behavior, but not changed significantly."
> "She has always been a warm, loving, understanding person."
> "He was wonderful before and fortunately there was no change—negatively."

The person described earlier as one who herself indicated that the retreat had had no effect whatsoever, was evaluated by a friend who wrote:

> No change—fortunately. She already had oceans of empathy for her fellow man, empathy resulting in action. Her Christian concepts have been so well developed that they are beyond the level of sensitivity proposed by the Shalom Retreats and her attendance made her more careful about the kinds of retreats she attends.

It seems worth noting that of the eleven evaluations which stated that no change had occurred, six were written by the spouse of the retreatant, one by the mother, one by a daughter, three by a friend. One couple evaluated each other as not changed. Ten persons of the eleven described as not changed, are married.

Some evaluators expressed ambivalence about the change they had noticed in a retreatant or they reported a shift from negative to positive change in behavior; others did not consider the change significant.

> "I'm sure this was a positive change for his personality—better for himself. But I liked him better as a sweet young guy. Now he's no longer milquetoast. He is firm in his stand and cannot be swayed" (a parishioner about her pastor).

A wife indicated that the change had been negative, "with indications of becoming positive."

> I don't know whether I can call this [change] significant; but he was helped somewhat; he says that he got some new insights.

There were several evaluations which described the change in behavior as only temporary. This was particularly the case for a considerable number of Albright students. We wondered whether young people were generally more critical in assessing other people's behavior than was the case for persons past their twenties. We also raised the question in our own mind whether the retreat had had less of an impact on the students because they had participated in it only on a semivoluntary basis and therefore had had less reason to work toward behavior change than older retreat participants who had come to Kirkridge out of a real need for further growth or change in attitude. Here are some comments made by fellow students about their friends who had gone to Kirkridge:

> "Until two weeks after the experience she felt she had all the answers in knowing how to best communicate with others. After contemplation, she realized that she does not have all the answers and that while her experience aided her in growing toward a better communication understanding, she still has a lot to learn and experience."
>
> "For a relatively short amount of time he seemed more well-adjusted and held a freer, happier outlook on life. It wasn't long, however, before he returned to the same attitude he had held before the encounter."

CHAPTER 5

The Follow-up Study

(Continued)

BEHAVIOR CHANGE—AS INDICATED BY CHANGES IN FIRO-B SCORES

We chose the FIRO-B test for our follow-up study because it deals with those aspects of interpersonal relationships which we intended to affect by the retreat experience. As William Schutz puts it so succinctly, "People need people to give to and to receive from."[1]

The test focuses on three different needs which all human beings have in common: inclusion, control, and affection. Schutz differentiates between behavior which we express toward other people—expressed behavior—and behavior which we want other people to show toward us—wanted behavior. This distinction can be illustrated by saying that I want people to be interested in me, to include me in some of their activities (wanted inclusion); I myself, on the other hand, am sufficiently interested in other people that I ask them to join me in pursuing a project (expressed inclusion). In the area of control I may wish to be controlled, told what to do, relieved of responsibilities (wanted control), or I may wish to be in a leadership role, "in charge," have power and influence over other people (expressed control). My affection need can manifest itself in my desire to establish emotionally close relationships with other people (expressed affection); if, on the other hand, someone wants to show love and affection toward me, I will not shy away from such expression of closeness (wanted affection).

Readers not familiar with the FIRO-B may be interested in a sample of the fifty-four questions. For each item six choices are given which range from "usually," "often," "sometimes,"

[1]William C. Schutz, *The Interpersonal Underworld* (Palo Alto, Calif.: Science & Behavior Books, 1967), p. 1.

"occasionally," "rarely" to "never." Here then are samples and in parentheses the need area with which each deals:

> I try to be with people (expressed inclusion); I like people to include me in their activities (wanted inclusion); I try to have other people do things the way I want them done (expressed control); I let other people strongly influence my actions (wanted control); I try to have close personal relationships with people (expressed affection); I like people to act cool and distant toward me (wanted affection).

A person can express any of these three needs in a deficient, excessive, or ideal manner. He may be undersocial (withdrawn) or oversocial (constantly seeking attention, believing in "togetherness," looking for companionship at all times). In the control area he may act like an autocrat (dominating, competing) or like an abdicrat (submissive, shunning all responsibility). As far as his affection needs are concerned, he may be underpersonal (emotionally distant, keeping his "cool") or overpersonal (wanting to be liked by everybody, constantly seeking intimacy or approval).

Both excessive and deficient ways of having needs met are based on insecurity (anxiety): a person is either constantly trying to have his needs met (excessive) or is trying not to have them met directly (deficient). The ideal manner of expressing his needs will bring their satisfaction.

In view of data reported in the previous chapter relative to changes in retreatants' self-image, it seems important to state that Schutz relates each need-area to one aspect of a person's self-concept: the inclusion need responds to the need to feel *significant and worthwhile*; the control need to the need to feel *competent and responsible*; the affection need to the need to feel *lovable*.

It was difficult to choose which of the extensive data to include in this chapter. Since the questionnaire as well as the confidential evaluation concentrate on changes in retreatants' behavior, attitudes, and feelings, I decided to make *the change in scores from test to retest* the main focus of this report about FIRO-B data. I proceeded as follows: the combined scores (wanted *and* expressed behavior) for each sector (inclusion, control, affection) were tabulated as either low, medium, or high (these levels have been determined by research: low scores range from 0-3, medium from 4-5, high from 6-9). I then compared the scores on the first test with those of the retest for each respondent. Seven different kinds of changes were possible and therefore assigned to each respondent: his score could either remain within the same category of low, medium, or high; it could increase from low to medium, medium to high, low to high; or decrease from high to medium, high to low, medium to low.

Schutz writes: "Seventy percent of the highs and lows remain in the same category on the retest, whereas half of the middles retain their status. *The probability of an individual's jumping from a high to a low or low to a high, is very slight—about 10 percent.*"[2] Using Schutz's figure as basis for comparison, special attention will be given to changes in scores from level to level, particularly from low to high and high to low.

A comparison of the total scores—inclusion, control, and affection combined—shows that 17% more Albright students (A-Group) than persons in the Kirkridge Group (K-Group) had scored high on Test I (Table A22). Twice as many persons in the K-Group than in the A-Group had scored medium while the number of persons scoring low was similar for both groups. On Test II there was an increase of 13 percent in high scores for the K-Group; for the A-Group the number of high scores remained the same. Many more students kept their scores at the same level of either low, medium, or high than was the case for the K-Group (57% vs. 47%). This data may once more point to the possibility that the retreat had less of an impact on the students than on other participants in Shalom Retreats as the students had come to Kirkridge only on a semivoluntary basis while many adults had a clearer idea of what they were hoping to get out of the retreat than was the case for the students.

We compared the total scores of *men* and *women* (K-Group only) and found that considerably more women had received a high score on Test I (42% vs. 26%—see Table A23). This difference does not surprise us too much since we can safely make the generalization that women on the whole tend to be more expressive of their emotions than men.

Medium and high scores increased for a similar percentage of men and women.

A look at the scores of *married* persons and those of *persons*

---

[2] Ibid., p. 79.

without spouse (the latter category included single, separated, divorced, and widowed persons) showed that 36 percent of the married people increased their scores versus 21 percent of those without spouse (Table A24). It seems reasonable to assume that a married person is more likely to learn and risk becoming more expressive of feelings and needs than a person who is alone.

Inclusion

Schutz describes the person who has no problem in the area of inclusion as "comfortable with people and comfortable being alone. He feels that he is a worthwhile, significant person and that life is worth living. He is fully capable of being genuinely interested in others and feels that they will include him in their activities and that they are interested in him."[3]

In the area of inclusion 49 percent of the K-Group scored low on Test I as compared to 29 percent of the A-Group (Table A25). While similar numbers of persons in both groups scored medium, there were many more students with high scores (57%) than there were in the K-Group (33%). Though one should beware of generalizations it seems nevertheless reasonable to state that acceptance by the peer group is very important to young people; their high inclusion scores may well lend support to this assumption. When Schutz compares the undersocial (see the high percentage of K-persons with low inclusion scores) with the oversocial (see the students) he mentions that the interpersonal dynamics may be the same for both kinds of people though their overt behavior is opposite. The oversocial as well as the undersocial fear that they will be ignored, that nobody will be interested in them. An indication that many of our retreatants felt more secure about themselves when they took Test II is seen in the fact that in the K-Group 17 percent more people scored high on Test II than they had done on Test I, while 18 percent fewer scored low; on the other hand, many students (21%) lowered their scores. This data may well point to the possibility that the sense of self-worth was indeed enhanced as a result of the retreat-experience; it may lend further support to statements made by retreatants as well as some of their significant others to the effect that a change in self-image had occurred (see chapter 4).

---

[3] Ibid., p. 27.

Considerably more *men* (42%) than *women* (26%) showed high inclusion needs when they took the test the first time (Table A26). There is no marked difference between men and women in terms of increases or decreases in their respective scores from test to retest. A closer analysis of the increases showed, however, that *a significant 18 percent* of both women and men had changed their scores *from low to high.*

Control

A person who has no problem in the area of his control needs is described by Schutz as feeling

> comfortable giving or not giving orders, and taking or not taking orders, as is appropriate to the situation. Unconsciously, he feels that he is a capable, responsible person and therefore that he does not need to shrink from responsibility or try to constantly prove how competent he really is. Unlike the abdicrat and autocrat, he is not preoccupied with fears of his own helplessness, stupidity and incompetence. He feels that other people respect his competence and will be realistic with respect to trusting him with decision making.[4]

In the control area the Kirkridge and Albright Group scored very similarly on Test I and Test II (Table A27). Both groups showed a higher percentage of decreases (K-Group 25%, A-Group 43%) than increases (K-Group 19%, A-Group 7%). This data may indicate that our retreatants' need to be dominating in their relationship to other people had diminished, that they had become better able to give other people the freedom to make their own decisions. A person whose anxiety about his competency diminishes has no doubt less of a need to be dominating in his relationship to other people.

We were interested to see whether control needs differ markedly among *men* and *women* (Table A28). A comparison of scores for these two groups among our respondents showed that 15 percent more men than women had scored high when they took the test the first time. At the time of the retest 10 percent fewer men scored high again while the number of women scoring at that level remained almost the same. It may well be that many of these men had no longer such a pronounced need to be dominant, controlling, or "in charge" when they took the test again many months after the retreat.

---

[4]Ibid., pp. 29–30.

On the other hand, the increase in number of women whose control score was higher upon retest seemed to point to the possibility that many of them felt more confident about their own competency, their capabilities, and their ability to assume responsibility. One evaluator described what he considered as indication of such a change in self-image as follows: "She is more expressive of her thoughts—less submissive and dominated."

When we compared the scores of *pastors* with those of *men of other professions* (K-Group only) we were startled to find that the number of pastors with high control scores was very much larger than that found among men of other professions (57% vs. 30%). On Test II the control scores decreased among more pastors (48%) than men of other professions (22%). The scores of 60 percent of nonpastors remained at the same level; for the pastors this figure was 43 percent (Table A29).

Affection

Here again we quote Schutz:

> For the individual who successfully resolved his affectional relations with others in childhood, close emotional relations with one other person presents no problem. He is comfortable in such a personal relation, and he can also relate comfortably in a situation requiring emotional distance. It is important to him to be liked, but if he isn't liked he can accept the fact that the dislike is the result of the relation between himself and one other person—in other words, the dislike does not mean that he is an unlovable person. Unconsciously, he feels that he is a lovable person who is lovable even to people who know him well. He is capable of giving genuine affection.[5]

Can people intend to love? Is the retreat an adequate means to help people experience and at last believe that they are indeed lovable? The following analysis of test data pertaining to the area of affection shows that people can indeed learn to take the risk of establishing close interpersonal relationships.

In comparing Test I and Test II we found on Test II 19 percent more persons in the K-Group and 29 percent more students in the A-Group scored high in the area of affection (Table A30). In both groups almost 40 percent increased their scores from low to medium, medium to high, or low to high. Of particular

---

[5]Ibid., p. 31.

significance is the finding that of the K-respondents *12.4 percent went from low to high.*

A very noticeable difference in affection scores emerged between *married persons* and *those without spouse* (K-Group only). While 22 percent more married persons scored high on Test II the percentage of persons in the other group remained the same; the single, separated, divorced, or widowed respondents distinguished themselves from married persons by scoring medium in far larger numbers on Test II than they had on Test I (increase of 13% vs. decrease of 8%). Among the married we found 41 percent who showed an upward change in score versus 29 percent of those without spouse (Table A31). The significant *low to high shift* occurred in *13 percent of the married persons.* The just-described differences between these two groups among our retreatants raise the question whether it may not be easier for married persons than for those without spouse to surface their affectional needs and to express them in their relationship to other people.

24 percent more persons scored high upon retest among those who had had *previous sensitivity training* as compared to 12 percent among those with no such previous experience (Table A32). The significant percentage who made the shift from low to high was found among the "experienced" (19%) as compared to 4 percent of the "inexperienced!"

A comparison between the affection score of *pastors* and those of *men of other professions* proved very worthwhile. When tested the second time 38 percent more pastors scored high than they had on Test I; for men of other professions the increase was 15 percent. It seems appropriate at this point to remind the reader of the previously reported finding obtained from questionnaire data that 95 percent of pastors had reported a change in their expression of the need to be loved as compared to 67 percent of men of other professions. In both groups around 14 percent made that significant change *from low to high* (Table A33).

The raw scores of both Test I and Test II do not lend themselves to particular analysis. They are shown in Table A34 and compared to the scores of two control groups which Schutz used for research purposes.[6]

---

[6]William C. Schutz, *The FIRO Scales* (Palo Alto, Calif.: Consulting Psychologists Press, 1967), p. 7.

Did most retreatants return home from the Shalom Retreat with a feeling that they had a mountaintop experience which would permanently influence some of their thoughts and attitudes regarding the life and mission of the church and their relationship to the local church? Would they try to suggest freer forms of worship, initiate new kinds of groups where some of the Shalom methods would be used? The following section will deal with answers to these questions, i.e., with data that we obtained from Part III of the questionnaire, the part which focuses on local church relationships.

In order to find possible differences between clergy and laity in the way they answered questions related to the church, we combined the Kirkridge and LaForet Groups and compared the responses of all the pastors with those of all the laymen. The eight respondents who indicated that they were not members of a church were not included as they had been asked not to deal with strictly church-related questions. The following data are based on a total number of clergy of forty-one and a total number of laity of eighty-seven.

Understanding the Meaning of Life or Religion

The question dealing with this issue read: "Has the Shalom Retreat had a lasting effect on your understanding of the meaning of life or your religion? Yes____ No____ (If yes, please describe.)" *90% of the clergy, 84% of the laity, and 86% of the Albright students answered this question affirmatively* (Table A35).

Here are comments made by the respondents to illustrate how they thought their understanding had been affected:

> "Helped me to see that God is asking me to be and unfold the unique me He created—to be with integrity and freedom. Life, my life, others' life, life in nature, is to be released and celebrated and offered. So the retreat has helped me to relax in this grace, this acceptance, this affirmation—free from 'shouldism' and 'oughtism' of the law. So both more life has been experienced and what life is to be is in clearer theological and personal focus."
>
> "The Shalom Retreat helped me to find a center that somehow had become buried through the years to the point where I had no direction, no real goals for my life. I have found new

meaning in life, knowing that I desperately need love from others and also in knowing that when I give love, I can give of myself, my special gifts to others who need me! This insight has profoundly hit me—that I really do need the love of every other individual I meet and he or she needs my love. But so often we get hung up on outward mannerisms and turn one another off. I *know* that I am more whole, more truly happy when I receive the love of another person and he receives mine. And there can never be too much love. To give and to receive love has given *new* meaning to my life."

The Mission of the Church

Though there was little "church talk" at our retreats we hoped nevertheless that many retreatants would return home with a deepened concept of the mission of the church. This hope led us to ask whether the Shalom Retreat had had a lasting affect on the respondents' understanding of the mission of the church. *88 percent of the clergy and 71 percent of the laity thought the retreat experience had influenced their view regarding the mission of the church* (Table A36). The Albright students could not be included as our pilot questionnaire did not deal with this particular issue.

> "I cannot separate the meaning I discovered for my own life from what I see as the mission of the church. Being freed up to live and feel life more deeply and feeling that the Holy Spirit was clearly present in a ministry of exorcism—says to me that this is what the church ought to be doing. Personally, I want to live a freer life and be a presence that frees others. As one committed to Christianity (or Christ, anyway!) I want the church to be that kind of presence in the world. The potential is staggering."
>
> "I now feel the mission of the church should be programming that will meet the needs of people and I am thinking particularly of the need for all people to know they are loved and accepted for who they are. I feel only as people feel love from others and God can they give of themselves."
>
> "The process, interaction, is more important than the product, 'perfect' people."

Acceptance of the Institutional Church

Month after month we read the theological reflections which the retreatants wrote toward the end of the Shalom Retreat. Could we doubt that many persons had seen a vision of what might be possible in the life of the local church in depth relationships, more creative worship or a different emphasis in the life of church groups? What effect, then, did the retreat have on attitudes toward the institutional church? We asked, "Do you find it easier____; same as before____; more difficult____ to accept the present state of the institutional church?"

10% of the clergy, 33% of the laity, 14% of the Albright students reported there had been no change in their attitude toward the institutional church. 32% of the clergy, 7% of the laity, and 21% of the students thought they found it easier, but *56% of the clergy, 54% of the laity, and 57% of the students considered it more difficult to accept the institutional church as it presently* is as a result of their Shalom Retreat experience (Table A37).

It was somewhat of a surprise to see that 32 percent of the clergy considered it easier to accept the present state of the institutional church. They commented:

> "I have reason to be more hopeful."
> "I am accepting church members 'where they are,' not where I think 'they should be.'"

Some persons indicated that their quarrels with the church had been of long duration:

> "I was disillusioned before the retreat!"
> "I've been disgusted with the institutional church since long before Kirkridge."
> "It simply is not meeting the needs of the people!"
> "It is more irrelevant to 'real' life than I thought."

The questionnaire then asked whether the retreatants had discussed their feelings about the institutional church with other members of their church and/or their pastor.

For clarity's sake the responses made by pastors' wives were grouped separately. Only 4-6 percent of either the pastors, pastors' wives, or laymen had *not* shared their feelings with their minister and/or other members of their church regarding the influence which they thought the retreat had had on their attitude toward the church (Table A38). It must be pointed out that 12% of the clergy, 23% of the pastors' wives, and 17% of the laity did not answer that particular question.

Attitudes of Laymen and Pastors Toward Each Other

There were clergymen at every retreat and some of them came to Kirkridge with members of their congregation. In the course of the retreat these pastors were very open and honest in expressing some of their intensely felt pain and/or anger about some aspect of their ministry. It was of interest to us to find out whether laymen's attitudes toward their own minister had changed as a result of what they had learned from the pastors at the retreat. Furthermore, we wanted to know whether they had told their pastor that they had been feeling differently about him since the retreat. *46 percent of the laymen reported a change in their attitude toward their minister; among them 66 percent had expressed this change in attitude directly to him* (Table A39).

Here are some of the laymen's quotes:

> "From seeing other pastors agonize with their problems I realized mine had problems also so now I can show him more love and understanding."
> "They are human and needy too."
> "He is trying so hard in the wrong way."
> "I realized that he had many of the same problems as lay people, that he really was 'one of us.'"
> "I wish he could be on a gut level with us."

The pastors were asked an almost identical question except it referred to their attitude toward their congregation. 88 percent of the pastors thought they did indeed feel differently toward their church people than they had prior to the retreat. Among these were 89 percent who indicated that they had communicated their change of attitude directly to some of their laymen (Table A39).

> "I felt like I wanted to level with them and to show them my own needs. At the same time I have become much more tolerant of them and willing to accept them for who they presently are."
> "I think I see the congregation more realistically. I don't expect overnight miracles. I no longer 'grade' my ministry by their response. I see them more as people instead of sheep and am more responsive to their feelings."

It seems clear that the methods used at the retreats have the potential to help clergy as well as laity overcome some of the blocks which hinder them from really loving each other and ministering to each other.

Celebration

The moments of spontaneous celebration toward the end of our retreats seemed very meaningful to many who participated in them. Would the impact of these experiences be strong enough to lead our retreatants to suggest similarly free worship services, and times of celebration in the local church? 88 percent of the pastors and 52 percent of the laymen had suggested to their home churches that freer forms of worship be experimented with. Of the clergy who had made such a suggestion 75 percent reported that it had been followed; for the laity this figure was 58 percent (Table A40).

Those who felt they could not even make the suggestion that their church experiment with freer forms of worship, put their discouragement quite bluntly:

> "The slightest deviation throws the old guard into panic."
> "I get a great sense of futility even thinking about any changes."

Applicability of Shalom Methods to the Local Church

As part of our research we checked how many retreatants had dealt with the question regarding the applicability of the Shalom methods to the local church, a question which we had suggested they deal with as part of writing their theological reflections. Among the Kirkridge Group we found that 52 percent of the clergy and 66 percent of the laity had expressed their view on this subject (nonchurch members were excluded in determining the percentage figure). An analysis of the content of their remarks showed that every one of the pastors and 66 percent of the laymen who had dealt with that question felt that the Shalom methods could be used in the local church. They expressed their hope and optimism in the following ways:

> "I do see hope in what we have done here for the local church. Indeed, if it or something like it is not put into earnest practice soon, I see little future for the church."
> "If I could find a church where the members relate to one another in a meaningful way, I would find it much easier to renew my commitment to the church. I would very much like to see these kinds of experiences in my church."
> "For the local church there is this hope, that by this method they will come alive—they will be open—they will learn to love in spite of all the risks—pain, suffering, and threats. Terrific way to meet conflict in the church."

But we hear also those who expressed pessimism and doubt regarding the usefulness of these methods to the church. It did not surprise us that the least hopeful statements had been made by some of the students.

> "I know that in the church back home, these methods would never work. The church leaders teach that you should be strong and bear all your burdens—that you should only unload them on Christ. Also, people are too concerned with church business to reveal their inner feelings and to let their hair down—they have to keep up their image."
>
> "I see the church as too antiquated to try anything as revolutionary as this. They are too satisfied with the status quo. I used to go to Church every Sunday and I would sit there and listen to the same old sermon, sing the same old songs, etc. I don't need that. I need something that I can relate to, people, the world. The world is my church; its people are my hope for the future. When you look at it that way, my church is crying out for this sort of thing and we really need it."
>
> "I wish I could run into my church right now, jump onto the pulpit and yell, 'Don't sing those damn hymns because they're part of the program; sing them because you really rejoice about your life! Just hold the people sitting on either side of you and love, love, really love them!"

New Groups in the Local Church

What had retreatants done upon their return to their local church? Had they started new groups modeled after the one they had experienced at a Shalom Retreat where people would be attempting to become more honest and open in sharing some of their real feelings? In order to get an answer to this question, we asked in the questionnaire: "Have you since the Shalom Retreat suggested or initiated any type of small group in which basic encounter methods are central? If yes, did you do this within the church? Are you at the present time participating in such a group? If yes, is this group related to the church?"

61 percent of the clergy and 36 percent of the laity suggested formation of such small encounter-type groups. Of those pastors and laymen who had made this suggestion, 71 percent (73% for the laity) had done so in their local church. 56% of the pastors and 34% of the lay people reported being in a small group at the time of the follow-up study; 83% of these pastors and 71% of these laymen participated in such small groups within their local church. It seems worth noting that the figures for the clergy are considerably higher than for the laity which means of course that a pastor can much more easily influence

what happens in his church than is possible for most laymen (Table A41).

It needs to be pointed out that quite a few persons who had not suggested the formation of a new kind of small group in their church nevertheless checked that they were actively participating in such a group at the time of the follow-up study. Quite a number of persons at our retreats were members of churches where encounter-groups were already very much part of the church's life.

There is no question in our mind that many persons returned to their church with the hope and desire to participate in a kind of group where they could continue to grow and where depth relationships would become possible. Those who wrote the following statements may well have spoken for many of our retreatants:

> "We would like to start a group but don't know how to go about it."
> "Our pastor is scared of this!"
> "How will I find others who feel as I do? From where will I receive the strength and support?"

We remain deeply concerned about the question of follow-up and of continuing groups for those who have participated in a Shalom Retreat. We know from our own experience that it takes effort, support, and encouragement from others to remain on the growing edge, to risk new kinds of behavior, to attempt becoming more honest in the expression of one's feelings and one's needs. We are very aware of the fact (see Table A41), that it is near impossible for the majority of laymen to bring off a different emphasis in the life of small groups in their church if they do not have their pastor's full support, if he himself has not experienced how Human Potential methods can help many people find greater depth in human relationships, fulfill their potential, and become more honest, trusting, and loving.

The Importance of Pastors

Before we end this report about the findings of our follow-up study, we would like to give particular attention to statements made by pastors and about them in questionnaires and confidential evaluations. We do this in the hope that other pastors will take seriously what colleagues had to say about changes in feelings, attitudes, and behavior attributed to their experiences either at Kirkridge or at LaForet.

Let us again point to data mentioned earlier which show quite clearly that pastors as a group were significantly influenced by their Shalom experience: compared to 67 percent of men of other professions, 95 percent of the pastors indicated that they expressed their *need to be loved* more than they used to. A parishioner, in her confidential evaluation of her pastor, described how he became more expressive of his feelings upon his return from the retreat. She wrote:

> He was a guy who never would let anyone really love him. He always stood off and put a barrier between those who wanted to love him and himself. Since coming back from the retreat he has shared for the first time in five years himself at a gut level and what he really does feel deep down.

Several pastors indicated that they had become more *vulnerable*, better able to share their feelings.

> "More free to express love; less inclined to preserve or protect my 'image.'"
> "I am able to operate more on a feeling level with friends and neighbors. Sermons, I believe, are more on a gut level."
> "A willingness to be vulnerable and allow church members to know my honest feelings."
> "Great desire to get closer to them emotionally and to ask them to see me as a person rather than a professional."

On the FIRO-B we found clear evidence that the pastors had indeed become *more expressive of affection*. When they took that test the second time 38 percent more pastors scored high affection, compared to 15 percent of men of other professions.

81 percent of the pastors as compared to 33 percent of men of other professions reported they had learned to deal with their *anger* in a more constructive way than they used to. As one laymen wrote about her pastor: "He expresses his anger but doesn't stay angry." And a pastor said about himself:

> (I am) "less hostile, more able to love them because I am less dependent on having my emotional needs met indirectly as they accept or reject my ideas. I know I'm loved and don't have to have it proved in these ways."

Handling of *conflict* seems related to the issue of anger.

Here is a comment made by a wife and one by a parishioner about pastors:

> "He is not as afraid of conflict as he once was."
> "Much more able to handle conflict in a loving, forgiving manner."

The FIRO-B revealed that the *control* needs in pastors had decreased much more than in men of other professions though it needs to be stated again that the pastors' need for control showed to be very much greater when they were tested the first time.

The following statements can be used to illustrate how some pastors' *professional abilities* had apparently been enhanced:

> "Freedom from bad feelings about himself has made him much more confident of his abilities and he is much more creative in his work at church."
> "The experience at LaForet has equipped me for the tasks that try and test the clergy and church today. My goal here right now is to help my congregation to become the loving and caring community it needs to be today."
> "I especially noticed in groups and in counseling I'm not as protective any more. I am not as upset by hostile expressions as in the past."

An interesting shift apparently occurred in the attitude of the pastor who wrote:

> I'm less interested in dealing with social issues on the level of information and education and instead think we have to deal with fears, etc., which control our acceptance of and use of information.

All these statements by and about pastors regarding changes which they themselves had observed or which were reported by their wives, parishioners, or colleagues leave us with a great deal of hope that more and more clergymen will risk becoming vulnerable, more willing to share their real feelings with their parishioners, and more open to receive the love which they need as badly as any other human being, the kind of love which cannot be earned but only received as a gift.

CHAPTER 6

Theological Reflections

We wondered how contemporary people interpret peak experiences in theological terms or in "meaning" terms if they are not religious. We wondered which theological themes would emerge: which would be dominant and which ones would be minor. We wondered whether contemporary people still see a relationship between depth experiencing and the biblical story. So we asked our Shalom retreatants.

On the last morning of the retreat, immediately after breakfast, we ask them to engage in theological reflection. Here are the simple instructions we give:

1. What new light does this experience shed upon any of the following:

your understanding of Christianity?
your faith?
the biblical story?

2. Do you see any implications for the local church? For example, do you think the methods used at this retreat are applicable there? Please write freely and spontaneously out of your feelings and perceptions. Do not try to be precise. If you can, do a stream-of-consciousness kind of writing.

As part of the verbal introduction each time we say something like this:

> The world has changed in radical ways. All major institutions in our society are being forced to update their style, which means the way they communicate and the way they act. The church is no exception. It matters what you think and how you express your meanings. You can help the professional theologians do their job. As a matter of fact, they can't do their job without you.

We received tremendous cooperation. Only one person in the entire series did not turn in a reflection. Each wrote in his own style. The reflections were mimeographed and distributed to the group after they returned home. Altogether we received over 120 single-spaced pages of mimeographed reflections.

Two strains: Two distinct strains of material run through the data. Some people chose to write in a very personal, immediate style:

> "I found release for some of my garbage."
> "I believe that a demon was exorcised."
> "I have renewed faith."
> "I feel very strongly that . . . "
> "During the celebration, God became very real to me."

Others spoke in a more objective style, seeming to distance the experience a bit more, though referring to some of the same realities as those who spoke more personally.

> "Grace is receiving something good—love . . . "
> "In the marathon each person is confronted with the need to give and receive love."
> "The call of God is highly personalized."
> "There is great need to bring these new freedoms into play in small close groups."
> "The church today is . . ."[1]

WHAT THEY SAID

Harvey Cox in his *Feast of Fools* says:

> We must see that the problem of the death of God is not merely an intellectual one. It is also intuitive and aesthetic. Men today do not simply complain that they cannot believe in God on intellectual grounds. Indeed a religious explanation of the universe may be just as conceptually adequate as another one. That is not the problem. The problem is that people do not "experience" or "encounter God." Religious language including the word "God" will make sense again only when the lost experience to which such words point become a felt part of the human reality.[2]

There is real evidence in our theological reflections that what Cox calls "the lost experience to which such words point" did indeed become "a felt part of the human reality" for many people on the retreats.

---

[1]The earlier retreats tended to produce more objective, impersonal data and the later retreats were proportionately heavy in personal, immediate data.

[2]Harvey Cox, *Feast of Fools* (New York: Harper & Row, 1969), p. 28.

In an essay called "Toward a Theology and Practice of Religious Experiencing," James V. Clark says:

> To state the central observation of the essay, the *mutually revelatory relation* is the medium in which all the central elements of religious experience emerge almost at once. These elements are a *revelatory experience*, the development of *transcendent values* such that the person values facing toward the content of his revelation, *faith* in Tillich's sense (1957) of developing an internal ultimate concern with the external ultimate seem only in symbols, and *witnessing*, by which I mean acting-moving toward or in some way expressing one's ultimate concern.[3]

As I have read and reread the theological reflections which emerged from our retreats, I sensed again and again the depth of religious experiencing which is apparent there. All four of the characteristics described by Clark are profusely evident.

We are sorry that we can only include in this chapter a small number of the reflections. We wish we could include them all for they are very beautiful. We want to honor the ones which we have selected as illustrative by letting them stand alone without further comment. They are powerful witnesses to religious experience in our time. They are not systematic theology but a kind of "doing theology" in the midst of experience. There is also here ample evidence that God-talk is not dead and that the symbolism of the biblical story still has great power to help people verbalize and interpret their depth experiences. A reader may wish to scan this chapter or read it only partially before going on. Another reader may wish to read part of the chapter, then after going on, return to finish.

The material is presented under *major themes* and *subordinate themes.*

MAJOR THEMES

I. God

Where is God? "God is love and God is every human being. That's where he is. Not in the sky. Love is quiet and strong and healing and there God is motherly and fatherly.

---

[3]From James V. Clark in *Challenges of Humanistic Psychology,* ed. James F. Bugental (New York: McGraw-Hill, 1967), pp. 255–56. Copyright 1967 by McGraw-Hill, Inc. Used with permission of McGraw-Hill Book Company.

"God is not angry at us (he may be angry at hate and hurt that separates us from him—this is our sin being separated from God's love)."

Serving God and man. "I cannot serve God (nay—love God) as an abstraction. I can only serve him as I love people. I can only receive God's love as I see and feel it in a person.

"I have prayed for years that God's love should be able to pass through me to others, but I kept getting in the way. I feel that a major channel has begun to open up from this marathon. I now pray that I will be swept clean with this love. It will be much harder than reading theology and nodding in agreement, but God, it is going to be great!"

"I have tried to teach about the Bible, faith and Christianity for years. I can now in a really new and honest way.

"The deal is unity and God is the organizer and he's in people. My tentacles are all over the place."

A joyful exclamation. "Now I know what Immanuel means. God is with us. He is not far off, a God of the past alone. His mighty acts still are. Christ *is* our redeemer or he never was. God is creating, bringing newness of life, or he never was the Creator in the first place. God is in the present, the here and now! Hurray! Alleluia!"

Confirmation at last. "YES, GOD IS LOVE! Now I know God is love. He has returned to me in this concept at last. My former concept during the past few years was—he was nothing. Now he is real.

"In Jesus I see the humanity of God. Jesus was fully, really, completely human. In his humanness he allowed all humanness and glorified man.

"The biblical story came alive as I saw Christ in human beings reaching out to Martha and Mary, to Lazarus, to Mary Magdalene, all of us with our human foibles, and sins and heartaches and strengths—Christ in me the hope of glory. Those Christ-persons have helped me to realize afresh that God's love in Christ has to be translated by human beings to human beings. And this is the miracle!"

II. Faith and Trust

Trust for people emerging. "The mist and the light wind and the bright leaves are holding us in this quiet world—I'm sure it's for the same reason that I've always held back from revealing what I feel very freely—because, as Jerry would say,

I'm afraid of producing just one little goat turd—somehow I've seen here a door out of that mess—I've never doubted the love of God. I didn't mind his seeing me drunk, sober, selfish, naked, proud, joyful, or anything. I suppose there's a kind of inevitability about God seeing you as you are anyway because I believe he's going to anyway whether I like it or not—so I might as well accept it—and frankly I've *never* felt judged. But people I haven't trusted—nor have I trusted the church of God—or his love through the church. The fact of the fantastic love that grew here between all of us—the freely given—full of laughter and empathy and anger—love is like a miracle. It is what I've always wanted to find in a church—a place where I could damn well be myself—and to hell with hiding. The knowledge that I can be loved without wearing a mask or that love is not withheld because I don't measure up—well I've simply never believed it. I believe it now because I felt it happen.

"I think with excitement about what this movement will mean—is meaning. At this moment, I feel very close to God. I'm sure he's been kicking around here all week-end."

Trust, a new and wonderful feeling. "My name is Grace. I never liked my name, I never really liked myself; I therefore was not free to love others. This led to an unconscious facade that could not be penetrated, and attempts at giving and receiving love ended in emptiness and frustration.

"Here I have first *felt*, really *seen*, and *heard* and been *touched* by other individuals. This led to a trust—a very new and wonderful feeling. With trust I dared to look at these facts of myself hidden to others as well as me. I dared to share these inmost feelings, becoming vulnerable to my fellow man. And that is when the miracle occurred. Seen in my imperfection, I was loved! Actually loved and accepted! No pretense, no apology, no earning—just openness and receiving—a gift freely given. Having received such a gift—I was set free. Free to love myself and others without demand or structure. My name is Grace! Praise the Lord!"

This is trust. "As I sit here, in this precious place with the love and peace seeping into all the empty and wounded areas of my life I feel whole. I see the beginning of a path outside the window—although I can see it only for a short distance. A heavy fog has shut out, closed off and actually taken away everything but the here-and-now and amazingly, I'm not afraid but really satisfied. This is trust! Because I've learned what redemption and reconciliation mean in a new sense for I have seen 'love one another as I have loved you' *in action.* I don't just know it in my head *but in my whole being.* I am part of the action in receiving as well as giving. I am realizing in very small part what it means 'to bear each other's burdens' and what Paul means when he talks of being set free."

One man's definition. "Faith is seeing God in others and in myself with the assurance that I am acceptable as I am—not only acceptable, but, *loved* and I am free to love and accept others as they *are.*

"Faith is the freedom to *be*—just as I am. Faith is the *joy* of living—the joy of feeling, loving, sharing to the fullest and this is the biblical Story—a glorious invitation to live life to its fullest with others."

Renewal of faith. "I have experienced love in this kind of Christianity instead of the old put-down of the Christianity I knew as a child. This kind will let me be free, to grow, to give, no matter what I am doing. I feel a renewal of faith. I plead with you, God, that you will not let this movement die but grow so that I may have love out in the world too—and that all people can share this beautiful experience."

My faith has been destroyed and now I'm free to grow. "Until today I never felt like a Christian—I felt to be less than perfect was to be less than a person. Now I see that being less than perfect is to be 'whole.' I've grown a milestone and I believe when God sees me now he says, 'It is good.' My faith has been destroyed and now it is free to grow. I believe in the *now.*"

III. Love

She got the message. "Christianity is a style of life—not a bag of carefully thought out and well preserved truths, handed down from generation to generation—memorized and repeated on Sunday morning. This style is simply *unconditional love.* There is no entrance fee to become a Christian. We can never get cleaned up enough or good enough to be eligible. All we have to do is accept the fact that we are loved. 'We love because God first loved us.' Love is undeserved, cannot be earned. In fact the harder we try to earn it, the more it eludes us. It is simply a gift. This is the *TRUTH,* 'Know the truth and the truth will make you free.'"

Love is! "Love is! That's what it's all about but you can't earn it. You receive it; it possesses you! You are seized by it, grabbed; if you give it a chance it'll wrestle you to the ground, even break your hip (Jacob) and hurt your ankle, but you don't mind—in fact you like it as a symbol of new life invading you. LOVE IS! It is as pervading as the perfumes of the earth, the warmth of the sun."

Let it in. "The new light shed upon my understanding of Christianity is that it really works but I see you've got to want love more than anything (more than your self-image, even more than your sanity) and when *all* else is abandoned and you lay stripped and empty and weak and sinful, the gift is given."

A new way of seeing. "I intend to love, love, love—first John because now he really wants and needs my love. He recognizes this need and accepts my love. Because he is able to accept love I feel it coming back on a real depth level. Before this retreat I was lonely and hungry for a depth relationship with him. Since I didn't have it and couldn't find it with him, I was empty—void, unable to give of myself to anyone. I feel like a whole person again. I feel like a person who will be able to start relating in a real way to people back home. My cup seems to be overflowing."

The empty package. "I grew up literally in the church. Perhaps because of this, I felt that I did not have to do a *searching out* for what faith meant to me. I was just there. Because I was there I was Christian—sort of an osmosis process—a very unquestioning process. I can see from this experience that I have not grown at all from this stage. I had made a nice, neat package and all my life have been putting scotch tape on any rips that appeared. The thing that really scares me—hurts me—this package that I have so conscientiously and lovingly taken care of is empty."

Love and the church. "The experience gives me a feeling for the concept 'love of God' which I had great difficulty with before. The group's love was not diminished by anger, reduced by time, goes with me when I leave, and at least in part preceded my coming. The love is an environment in which I live. All of these things have been traditionally said of God's love—but made little impact on me until this group experience.

"So . . . maybe the love of God (and/or Holy Spirit) comes only through human mediators such as this group. Traditional religion has emphasized the individual and his relationship to

God. That never meant much to me. I never experienced God, never knew what those words were supposed to mean. I think my Christian education was bassackwards. An experience like this should have preceded the first word concerning religious ideas, the concept of God.

"Obviously the community that can deliver a love that is similar to or identical with that of God, must be the church. Traditional church life is bankrupt. This experience was of the real church and the real Pentecost."

God is love—we are love. "God is love—we are love, I am love. I am now a man—a human man who gives, takes, whose cup is full. But will be drained and will be filled with love of life and love of love.

"This retreat has been the most rewarding Christian experience in my life—I am a Catholic."

Love won't run out. "To be able to share at the level we have is tremendously faith-building for me, and helps me know more than ever that I need to—want to—and can trust; that I have something to give and a need to give it—because the reality of the experience of faith grows by the sharing or giving away of it—and that I don't have to fear any more that the love may run out, that there isn't enough for me, that it won't be received. All my fears seem puny in the light of the power of love that has flooded this weekend."

A steady stream of love. "This Kirkridge experience has affirmed my previous understanding of Christianity, that it is love, love, love, that is undemanding, nonjudgmental, liberating. My head trip on Christianity is settled in my gut and I feel some surprise and a great deal of peace and assuredness that Christ's love is all it's cracked up to be. Instead of bits and snatches of love that didn't hang around long enough with me to allow me to take it in for what it was, this weekend has been one steady stream of love that affirms one's personhood. Such concentration of love was like an oasis in the desert for me and I've been roaming the sands knowing it was there and I had to find it."

I can be loved. "I finally realized really for the first time that I can be loved no matter what. That means I don't have to try so hard any more to please God-knows-whom and I don't have to feel guilty about not being perfect. I can believe that God loves me because I need him—*he* surely can do this if my house church friends are able to. It makes me realize what a precious gift my Christianity is—it offers me what I desperately crave—unconditional love. It offers me endless opportunities to see my world with meaning."

IV. Church

Anger and a vision.

"I feel angry—I feel angry.
I feel angry with the church.
It screwed me up!
As a child it taught me guilt
In the name of God!
It served to teach me worthlessness.
It gave me a wilderness and called it LOVE.
As a young man, yearning to LOVE
To serve that I might be served,
It rejected me!
I closed the door, to search anew.
I feel LOVE! I feel Joy!
GOD IS LOVE
LOVE IS GOD
WHAT A REVELATION
JESUS IS ALIVE!"

"The church as I know it, needs this kind of juice, now. 'Wherever a few are gathered together in my name'—this is what is needed. Gather small groups together in any and every church to learn how to love."

A vision of the church. "I have been in churches but this time a church was in me—the power of a love that lets people reach and dig with complete security and faith that the love will not fade or tarnish gives the human soul so much freedom it can ache with pain and shout with joy. And it's for everyone, anyone, and most of all the you(s) and the me(s) because that is where life is."

Anger at the institution. "I write this from the perspective of my membership in the Anglican Church, a church that I find cold, bleak and overly concerned with 'trappings,' ceremony, order, regularity, and nothing seems to relate to *me* as I am—I'm not talking about the friendships I have established in the church—I have many good friendships that have come about because I have involved myself in our church—it's the damned institution that really gets me uptight and the importance that's placed on bricks, mortar and ceremony. Cold and nonrelevant usually. I'm looking for something that just hasn't been there and I don't see coming there and that scares me. That's how I see the church and I guess I've failed to help change direction in the church—the problems are overwhelming if you get in there and listen—I'm still hanging in there but without any good feelings about where we're going."

A vibrant vision. "The church in the beginning must have been a community of love like the one we found here, a community where people could confess their sins one to another without fear that the knowledge of their sins would be used either as a weapon of destruction or a means of control, a community where love for one another meant ability to trust and the knowledge that when you hurt your fellowmen hurt with you and could feel the pain, when you were filled with joy everyone else was filled with joy."

Some mixed feelings. "The church in many dresses I have looked at and felt some since childhood, since my mother's loving lullabies about God's love, to the awe and sensuous feelings of the Catholic Church's appeal to the senses of smell in incense, to sound in the ding-a-ling of bells and the rustle of robes. I could work up an anger against all the organization in churches but I'll leave that to others—I see her on her knees bent and bloody in our head-tripping society; I don't know how much I can do to help her; I care but I don't know if I care enough; perhaps she has to convince me that she is worth saving."

The new church emerging. "I am excited about this new church. This community of *Love* must continue for me or I will feel there is no church. My cup of pain was full and running over. Now my cup is filled with Love and I want it to spill over into every area of my life. Thank God! Thank God! Thank God!"

V. Community

Living and feeling. "This marathon experience was the actual living and feeling of the 'community.' It enabled me to experience love and acceptance in a new way."

Communities of being. "The church is also throwing around the words 'community' and salvation. These elusive terms have started to take on substance for me. Lots to say about building communities that do not depend on mood or function, but which recognize the need to *be* for one another. Yeh! The courage to be—*communities of being.* Church does too much talking and isn't available as a community of being. Given a community where 'two or three are gathered together in my name' Jesus Christ can still carry on his healing redeeming work."

New possibilities. "The Shalom retreat pictured to me on a feeling level the possibilities of reworking new ways of establishing real community. It showed us how important knowing is in loving.

"Christianity is a community faith—that which is not given and received freely cannot be love."

VI. Freedom

Vicarious suffering and freedom. "There *is* something like vicarious suffering (stell vertretendes Leiden) possible in the church and by the church. Some of us went through harder fighting and struggling than others. But—I feel—all of us experienced being freely the one who just here and now was fighting his battle. Each battle was a very personal battle and at the same time a battle for all who were present and together with all who were present. It also was a battle which the church is fighting for the world. Liberation became real to us, a frightening and at the same time a good and healing and creative experience."

A new freedom. "For years I've been trying to 'figure out' what I think theologically, always fearing that I'd be wrong or fail to see an error in my thinking, always avoiding an affirmation of any theological system and particularly any one church or faith. At the same time there's been a hunger for something definite to hang on to, to be mine—the security of a system is what I needed and wanted and feared never finding. I now feel a freedom and sense of peace about this whole area of thinking and feeling out a system. I've always known that love was the message of Christianity but I had never grasped the simplicity of it—it really *is* the message. It's not so complicated as I thought. I don't have to read 50 books on it and study all the religions of the world, read all the agnostic and atheistic viewpoints, be very intelligent or find someone perfect I can trust intellectually to think it out for me."

Freedom and style. "I'm not sure I even like the word Christianity any more because it reminds me too much of buildings, budgets, hierarchies, and all that junk that has kept us from being the church. But when I get beyond that it becomes people who are freed up by the Jesus life style, freed to no longer just talk about it, but to actually minimize the talk and do it, to live it where it's at—in the guts of people, because that's where God is, and that's where the Holy Spirit is, that's where this man, this loving man, Jesus, is."

"For tomorrow—freedom to risk complete trust in others, greater freedom to speak the truth in love, freedom to be sensitive to the pain, anger in others and to put aside one's own pet project for that moment."

I'm free. "I came here afraid! Uptight, but warm in Christianity. I laid in bed last night saying to myself, I'm free, I can go home to my wife and son and show them the love they really need and the love I've had for them so long and didn't know how to express."

Catharsis and freedom. "Catharsis is confession of sin and sin is a state of being rather than an act. Confession, and receiving forgiveness free me to love."

My freedom and the other's freedom. "I have gained a new insight to the meaning of freedom. I have had my own freedom—but giving freedom unequivocally is another thing. I realize as I never did before—that you cannot fully love unless you trust the individual enough to let them have their freedom. Keeping someone else in bondage and the degree to which you do it, is a real advertisement of one's own insecurity."

OTHER THEMES

Resurrection

Like a thread of gold. "Resurrection has again and again been affirmed these days of retreat. It has run like a thread of gold through each experience bringing with it the hope, the joy, the glory we can find right here on earth."

Resurrection is for real. "I know now that the resurrection is for real. This afternoon we will witness a group of whole new people leaving here carrying 'the Light' back to their respective areas of influence. The New Testament is portrayed here in its sincerity, in the feeling that we have for each and every one; as each person hit the pad 'the walls of Jericho' tumbled for the individual concerned. The final word in this episode is a four-letter word that doesn't get much attention in the press—LOVE."

Rebirth

Twice born. "We are 'twice born,' perhaps it is part of the condition of being a self-conscious human. First time we are born into dependence, into a family; the second time born to Freedom—the freedom to be ourselves, to relate to others as ourselves, to give ourselves to others."

Rebirth. "I feel a rebirth here that I would have thought impossible. But in this room and in these days we have lived out the biblical story, all of the blood, sweat and tears of being human and the agony of transformative suffering and the miracle, the ecstasy of rebirth."

Pilgrimage

Home lost and home regained. "For years the Bible has been to me a story of home lost and home regained with all the painful journey shared by a bunch of pilgrims in between. I have just had this deepened. The travelers can help each other so much more than I have originally thought."

Salvation

"What must a man do to be saved?—a question that comes up again and again and again can be reinterpreted as *What must I do to be human*? For me, I continued to raise it and then ran like hell and as I ran I heard footsteps and thought some people were out to get me and I screamed and yelled and cried in my fear and they ran up beside me and some said, 'I heard you, I heard you, take my hand—I want to run with you'; others said, 'I have a feeling you need to hurt yourself by running. You could stop you know and turn around and look at what you think is chasing you.' I said to myself they must be lying as soon as I stop they'll take advantage of me again. I raced harder and harder—and the people stayed with me and I was aware I was getting tired and then I began to feel the touch of the hands and the power of the words and I slowed down and began to turn around. I was so shaky after running so—trembling and breathing hard, and I realized I was so hot that I began to take off my clothes—each layer clung to me and was so painful to throw away and I cried, and I got angry at myself, and I ended up flat on my back on the ground—exhausted, relaxed and I turned around and found there was nothing to run away from. But the people who ran with me were there and we experienced love together and then got up to walk down the road of life arm in arm and that was pure JOY!"

RETELLING AND RELIVING THE BIBLICAL STORY

This section is of particular interest because of our hypothesis that intensive experiences utilizing Human Potential procedures can be understood in terms of the biblical story.

Many passages recalled. "The biblical story for me has been confirmed. I am more convinced of its truth and validity. I am grateful for those disciplines which hid it in my heart. Many passages were recalled during the experience. They were given meaning—flesh and bones. I'm glad we did not apologize for the moments of recall."

Acres of it came alive. "I shall have to think much about the Biblical story but at present I can say that it has brought acres of it alive. I can better see the 12 as diversified individuals and yet all experiencing each others' love. . . . Driving demons out is not a spooky and mystifying experiencing anymore. . . . Tears (Jesus wept) can be a manly experience and I feel closer akin to them. . . . Hate and anger are akin to love and must be dragged out and stomped on so that the vessel can be filled with only LOVE."

Reenactment of biblical story. "In a very real sense the Shalom community is a reenactment of the biblical story. It is a historical reality—people loving people, calling the dead back from the grave, giving new life, receiving new life, healing wounds, helping the blind to see, feeding the hungry."

Still afraid. "I now want to know more about the biblical story although I am still afraid that it will rear up and push me down. I would like to be able to study it with a group such as this so that I would have the strength not to be defeated in my fantasy of fear about what much of the Bible is saying."

Biblical parallel. "I have found many parallels between the experience of this weekend and the biblical story. Although sin has not been labeled, it has been forgiven. Devils have been called out and love put in their place. We have all become brothers and sisters by seeing each other as humans like ourselves. We have torn down walls and laws and written a new law on each of our hearts. We have been strengthened out of revealing our weaknesses. To me, this is the good news and the message of Christ."

Taking the scriptures seriously again. "This is the same loving community I am sure that the early church had. I can just visualize Jesus hugging and loving his followers, Martha and Mary and those with whom he came in contact—those who would allow him and reaching out in love to those who would not, yearning for these persons. We are finally starting to take the scriptures seriously again. Devils have been chased out right here. People healed, body, soul and spirit. We are again recognizing that we are one rather than separate. One within ourselves, one with each other and one with God."

Tremendous religious experience. "I felt the retreat was tremendous religious experience for me, because it better taught me to love others. Seeing all my friends crying and frustrated gave me much pain, but seeing them really relieved gave me a joy of which power and importance I may never know. There was no falsity here; everybody and everyone was real. I believe I am a more religious person now than I ever was before. I cannot say for sure, however, that my belief in God has been reassured. I really believe that it has been, but I will need several months, perhaps years to know for sure."

Forgiveness. "To me the entire retreat was the living GOOD NEWS, with laying on of hands, confession, forgiveness, joy and pain, fear turning to trust, deliverance from devils, a manifestation of the gifts and fruits of the spirit, and a powerful presence of the Holy Spirit.

"There is much here for the church but it has to come through our behavior rather than our words."

The beloved community. "This weekend experience reaffirmed some truths in living, breathing color. The beloved community came to life. The names and faces were new but only for a short time. Then love came and made the people the caring and concerned ones. There were no barriers here. The age, the experience, the profession, the problems, and needs—none of these mattered. Our humanness alone counted. And God's all encompassing, renewing, forgiving love was manifested in our midst. Miracles unfolded before our eyes. Demons were cast out. Anger and fear and pain were laid bare and from this labor new spirits were born. There were givers and receivers and a combination of both. We risked enough to be vulnerable, to agonize, to weep, to reach out, to bind up, and to rejoice together."

Not just past history. "The biblical story speaks to me in a very different way now—something that speaks to me and applies to my life today and not something that is past history."

CHAPTER 7

Analysis of Theological Reflections

INTRODUCING DR. RUNYON

In anticipation of writing this chapter and with the sly hope that we might appear wiser than we are, we asked Theodore Runyon, professor of theology at Candler School of Theology, Emory University, to comment on the theological reflections and on the underlying process which produced them. We hoped thereby to glean some jewels which, properly recut, might sparkle on the pages of this chapter. But what he produced was of such excellent quality that we decided to use much of his material instead, just as he wrote it. This device will provide a certain evaluative objectivity and a theological viewpoint from one who has no reason to be protective of the data.

We find ourselves much in agreement with his very helpful perspective. Where we agree we will keep silent, except to add illuminative material from the theological reflections. Where we disagree in part we will say so and will add certain material of our own. The material of Professor Runyon will appear in italics; and our own in bold-face type. Those who wish to read Dr. Runyon's comments without interruption need only read the italics.

GOALS OF SHALOM RETREATS

As reflected in the statements of the participants, these retreats center on growth of the self through increased awareness of the self in all its aspects. A context of trust is developed in which negative elements can be shared with the group and thus purged from the individual, leading to a new sense of self-acceptance, freedom, and joy, which allows the self to move out in affirmation (love) toward others. To this extent there are parallels between Shalom Retreats and other groups within the Human Potential Movement. However, there is an added dimension here. Most of the retreat participants come out of churches and return to churches. This could provide a continuity between the retreat experience and continued nurturing in the local church. I perceive the retreat leadership as concerned about this question of how to preserve and develop the retreat experience once the participant has returned to his local church context. An attempt is made in the retreat to revitalize biblical language and symbols by using them to interpret and give authority to the central experiences of freedom and love.

THE CONTEXT OF THE EXPERIENCE: THE ENABLING COMMUNITY

While the self and its development is clearly the focus of the weekend that development cannot take place apart from a special kind of community which plays the indispensable role of enabler. The sociology of knowledge (cf. Berger and Luckmann, The Social Construction of Reality*) has demonstrated how the individual is guided and supported in his knowledge of reality, society and himself by the social conventions which undergird and verify his belief patterns. The retreats provide a temporary, volitional community, a covenant community, in which persons voluntarily join together for a short period of time to achieve certain goals. The brevity of the relationship has some definite advantages: (1) One is not likely to have to deal with most of the persons in the group again; therefore, honesty about oneself is permissible without as much danger of later embarrassment and regrets. (2) Intense openness to others is easier on a short-term basis than where the relationship will have to be maintained over a long period. The disadvantage, of course, is that the community is atypical, and therefore not immediately applicable to the situation of the local church, especially in the small town. The effort to have at least two persons who are long-term associates attend together is one way to counteract this disadvantage.*

The conjecture is reasonable and natural that the temporary nature of the community should lead to greater openness, since the people will probably not see each other again. However, we no longer believe that it is correct. It fails to take

into account the trust and love that develop in the group and does not take into account that the covenant of confidentiality is really honored. In cases in which groups have come together we have noted no great hesitancy to get into the group process and our follow-up of these persons in their own communities after they have returned has indicated a real sense of life together. Three pastors in a church in Annandale, Virginia came on separate occasions to a Shalom Retreat with some of their church people. Resistance to the opening up process because they already knew one another was not noticeable. Members of a church in Binghamton, New York who came with their pastor found no difficulty with the process and found their life together deepened. Relationships with friends who come from our own local church have been much enriched. In those cases where the pastors have come with their people we have found a real willingness to open up, both on the part of the pastor and the people and a deepening of that love and trust relationship once they returned home. Also we have real evidence that people want to stay in touch. Community does not take a long time to build. When there is trust there is openness. I make this point because the belief that people who live in close proximity cannot be open tragically keeps much local church life superficial.

The covenant community becomes in this context the agent of grace. Through these contacts, through the Word which comes to him from the whole community, not just the leaders (important as they are for setting the tone of that Word), individuals receive absolution, acceptance and love, which provide the basis for their new sense of freedom. Bonhoeffer's comment is here clearly illustrated;

> *God has put this Word into the mouth of men in order that it may be communicated to other men. God has willed that we should seek and find his living Word in the witness of a brother, in the mouth of man. Therefore, a Christian needs another Christian who speaks God's Word to him. He needs him again and again.*[1]

In a time of the breakdown of authorities, the group of which one is a part still has immense authority. Indeed, its authority

---

[1] Dietrich Bonhoeffer, *Life Together,* tr. J. W. Doberstein (New York: Harper & Row, 1954), pp. 12 ff.

has probably increased due to the vacuum left by the undermining of more abstract, ideational and institutional doctrines and values. The Word of absolution and self-worth declared by the community to the participant is not a different Word than he has heard in the context of his local church before. Yet it now becomes believable. *Why? Because the word in church was usually an abstract word about an abstract God. And here it becomes an incarnate word on the lips of other persons whom he is beginning to learn to trust. He cares how they feel about him. And when they declare their affirmation of his existence despite his ambiguity, that Word carries authority. Moreover, that authority, in the Christian context, is grasped as declaring an ultimate Word, one from a source which cannot fail. And it is not surprising that for many this becomes the first time they experience what previously has been largely theoretical with little real impact on life.*

The difference between the abstract word in church and the incarnate word on the lips of other persons and expressed by bodies in relation is the difference between night and day. This is probably the most important word for the church to hear—UNTIL WE CAN INCARNATE IN OUR LIFE TOGETHER THE WORD WHICH IS SPOKEN, IT DOES SCANT GOOD TO SPEAK THE WORD. To my mind no renewal of the church is possible until the community enfleshes the word that is spoken.

The community also encourages the expression of feelings of joy and release in co-celebration. Inhibitions are relaxed where expressions of emotions are permitted, and participants are enabled to enjoy their religion in a way impossible in most middle-class white congregations.

This is part of an overall pattern of catharsis and expression which the rules of the game allow and encourage, and which releases the person to experience himself and the reality of the world in quite new ways. Apart from the enabling role of the community this could not happen.

It is an exhilarating experience to watch people unfold. It is sad to realize that the strictures of our society box us in and our churches talk of joy, allow us to hear scriptures about joy, sing songs about joy but limit us so severely in expressing it with

our bodies and our souls in an unrestrained fashion—giving the spirit wings.

THE CENTER OF THE EXPERIENCE: SELF-AFFIRMATION

Self-doubt and identity-uncertainty are widespread in the rapidly changing society, and any approach which can tackle effectively problems such as these is bound to win acceptance and appreciation. The increase of a sense of self-acceptance and self-worth seems to be a primary goal of the retreatants. New sense experience, new sensations and self-awareness, are not sustaining unless accompanied by a positive change in one's view of himself.

This change is the result of a process in which one exposes himself as he understands himself to be (confession), and then waits to see how others respond to his self-image. This willingness to confess usually arises only when in some preliminary way a word of grace has been heard, which says that it is safe to confess (prevenient grace?) and tentative trust is established. This is the willingness both to trust the group to handle-with-care one's own self-image, and also to trust the Word coming from the group as a legitimate divine Word, i.e., one which ultimately wills life and not death.

GUILT, CONFESSION, AND ABSOLUTION

There is no question, however, that many participants have indeed experienced the Word of absolution, which has meant for them freedom from destructive self-doubt and a new sense of self-worth and life affirmation. They are able to see that the recognition of one's ambiguity results neither in the loss of one's self nor rejection by others, and, as a result, they are better equipped to cope with continuing ambiguity, needing neither to ignore it nor to rationalize it away, because the ambiguity can be seen in a larger affirmation context. Reconciliation with oneself is therefore possible:

> *"I'm really beginning to feel from the others here what I should have felt from the Trinity before—that I'm loved, not for what I do, but just because I exist."*
> *"I feel that I've broken from my shell for the first time, and can say from a gut level, 'I am good.'"*

> *"This discovery makes me so happy—I think I'll give myself a bear hug."*
> *"I feel more 'me' with this group . . . than I ever have in my life."*

This experience of being affirmed and affirming oneself makes it possible in turn to move out to affirm others. A security is provided which makes risking possible, since it is no longer necessary to expend all one's energies in protecting himself.

These further quotes from the theological reflections bear out Runyon's assessment of what is experienced on the retreat.

Unashamed

"To experience sensuous feelings as a gift—unashamedly and without guilt in the presence of God is a breakthrough."

"Love of man and woman—wholesome, without guilt due to lust."

Hiding

"This experience made me realize how much guilt and ill feelings are stored up in each one of us. When I was on the mat, I tried to hide my face and I just discovered that when I was out there, I couldn't hide from anyone. This applies to God. A lot of times I think I tried to unconsciously hide from him."

Learning All Over Again

"Somehow it's a matter of learning all over again how to proclaim such a gospel, leaving out all the old words with all their punitive guilt-making associations."

"Having lived among these resurrections makes me feel to hell with fear and shitting on myself and guilt and all that crap. Jesus saves—even me."

Forgiveness

"Although sin has not been labeled it has been forgiven."

"I have experienced forgiveness for the first time in my life."

No Guilt

"I've been (and feel no guilt either on this score) learning to feel my emotions as a woman."

Not Being Perfect

"I don't have to try so hard anymore to please 'God-knows-whom' and I don't have to feel guilty about not being perfect."

FRESH THEOLOGICAL DEVELOPMENTS

1. God-language

What is evident is not so much something new as an illustration of how the collapse of traditional God-language need not mean the end of religious experience. The dominant mood here is as old as Schleiermacher. Though the transcendent God "out there" may be obscure, religious experience is close at hand, and what we know in this experience is as near as we will ever get to God, and is indeed a participation in the reality of God. An implicit Kantianism is present in many statements: we do not know God in himself, but we do know our experience—which is enough.

In some cases there is a further reduction, a Feuerbachian collapsing of the subject into the predicates. This is also characteristic of the current theological scene (VanBuren, Herbert Braun). Examples from the reflections: "God is people." "Each person born has his belly full of love, which is God." "God is the giving and receiving of love between persons."

2. Identification with the Humanity of Jesus

The groups appear to be made up largely of more or less committed Christians who want traditional symbols revivified. ("The leaders' Christian emphasis made me feel safe and free.") Jesus continues to have authority for them and the affirmation of his humanity becomes a means of reassurance concerning, and affirmation of, one's own humanity. "Jesus had feelings—hugged Martha and Mary, had balls, expressed anger."

Whereas Christ's redemptive power has usually been associated with the power of his divinity or his ability to divinize his followers (cf. Augustine: "God became man in order that man might become God"), here we see instead a parallel to the current theological insistence that Christ's divinity is his humanity, and his humanity his divinity. If Jesus was human then it is O.K. to affirm humanity; we don't have to apologize for it. "There is Good News: it's really true that I'm O.K.—you're O.K."

3. Exorcism

The emphasis found here is not new, but has been neglected. It was certainly present in the revivals, with their emphasis on uncleanness and self-loathing, followed by cleansing, release, and purification. The sense of being washed clean, and the new peace and assurance which came thereby, are familiar themes. The fact that this theme strikes such a responsive chord with most groups is probably an indication that we are still largely a "guilt culture" rather than a "shame culture." Internalized and unresolved guilt still plagues many. The question which does not seem to be raised, however, is whether guilt does not have some value. *The whole effort seems to be to wash away guilt feelings and to castigate institutions and persons who have caused guilt.*

It is questionable whether persons would refer so often to exorcism if the leaders did not mention it, but it is significant that it is latched onto with alacrity and that the symbolism is undoubtedly very meaningful.

I want to mention briefly here how I perceive the "casting out of devils" has come to play a seemingly important part in the symbolism of the retreat. We are concerned primarily about the feelings of fear, anger, and pain which most of us have been programmed to deal with in a less than direct fashion and which block off experiencing of love and joy. These feelings are unresolved in the person and exist there in a unique way and in differing measure. As the person gets in touch with the fear, anger, or pain one can literally watch the expression of the feeling move from the mouth, to the throat, to the chest, to the belly. Many people simply give their whole body and spirit up to the feeling. We then can rightfully say, not "you are angry" but "you are anger"; not "you have pain" but "you are pain"; not "you are afraid" but "you are fear." One can see in this kind of experiencing what it means to be possessed by a devil, to get the person to scream it out, weep it out, beat it out, whatever seems most appropriate. When the person is through he is spent and exhausted. The person knows the "name" of his demon and can therefore control

him. The feeling is that of having gotten rid of a massive burden. The biblical symbolism thus really comes alive in this context. "A devil has been cast out." The symbolism is used not in a doctrinaire or literal sense but in the light, descriptive, symbolic sense.

The analogy to what used to go on in revivals, and in some areas probably still does, is a fair one and we believe that just as the revival was a "right" form for a particular time and then fell into disuse, God's spirit may use these new methods now in the same way.

The word guilt is seldom used in the course of the retreat, neither by the leaders nor by the retreatants. It is probably true that if the leaders made frequent use of the term this might also elicit use on the part of a number of retreatants. But it is probably significant that the term is seldom, if ever, used. Many people get in touch with strong guilt-related feelings, such as "I'm no good."

4. Experience as an Important Dimension of Meaning

Meaning has been understood as a largely rational and ideational phenomenon, associated with doctrine, symbols, and traditions. This is true even of more existentialist orientations (cf. Bultmann's "self-understanding" and his programme of demythologizing). We need to be reminded that little is meaningful to us unless it is accompanied by meaningful experience. Here Maslow's contribution is apparent. This has all kinds of implications for the way we go about Christian education.

> *"The church must shift from* telling *the good news to participation in the good news on a* feeling *level."*
> *"I think my Christian education was bassackwards. An experience like this should have preceded the first word concerning religious ideas, the concept of God."*

I will deal with this important emphasis in the last chapter. There probably is not a more important aspect of our work with and reporting about Shalom Retreats than this point made by Dr. Runyon in his paragraphs above. In the church we really have believed that the organ of salvation is the ear. We really did believe that people could hear "the word of the Lord" from the mouth of the preacher. But now we are learning that unless that word is enfleshed in the community for whom the preacher speaks, unless with one's whole self, body, and soul one can experience the truth of the words, the words are unheard. The barren and stilted love life of many churches simply ex-es out the word of the gospel. He is right—"meaning emerges from meaningful experience." Our children in Sunday school cannot hear the word unless that word comes to them in the context of the loving community that enacts the truth we want them to hear.

Maybe we can return to a kind of experiencing in the church which will draw others to it because they are able to say again, "Behold, how those Christians love one another."

5. Tactile Communication

Shalom Retreats share with the Human Potential Movement a heightened awareness of the importance of the sense of touch. The emphasis is not just on the discovery and acceptance of one's own bodily nature and feelings but the use of touching and embracing to communicate. Communication has usually been divided into verbal and nonverbal, but seldom has nonverbal explicitly included the sense of touch. Yet these reflections indicate that this can be an effective way for basic Christian meanings to be transmitted. The use of the body to communicate could be thought of as an implication of the doctrine of the incarnation. However, it would be difficult to ground this either historically or biblically. (Perhaps for that reason it qualifies as a new development.) The closest historical parallels would be the sacraments of anointing and the eucharist, if the elements are understood to transmit the eucharistic body of Christ. A contemporary parallel would be the "passing of the peace," taken over from the Church of South India liturgy.

I think these quotes from the theological reflections give ample evidence that Runyon is correct. Evidence is really here that tactile communication can be an effective way for basic Christian meanings to be transmitted.

Touch—A foretaste of heaven. "Hell is being alone, wandering alone in the dimensions, not being able to be at one with God and all the other souls.

"I think this explains why physical contact and a close, physical touching expression of love is so pleasant.

"This is the nearest we can come to heaven in this universe, since we are imprisoned inside our bodies, not free to touch everyone at once, but able to touch only a few at a time.

"It is a foretaste of heaven."

Love is a closeness. "Where did it all come from? and why not sooner? Will it last? When will it come again? For years, for all of us, I guess, it's been NO! DON'T! and now it's YES! and DO! Love is a closeness—no conditions, no overtones—no limits on when, how much, or toward whom. A delicious sensuousness to be enjoyed, not reserved, to be had, not just to be given."

"It's not very chic these days to exhibit too much of the spectrum of our emotional capability; one should be in control of one's feelings. The nerve endings like any other part of us atrophy with lack of use and one soon can't feel anymore—it becomes normal and we die a little."

Hugging as a medicine. "A whole person—I *feel* like a whole person—there's real healing in the warmth of loving and being loved. I've learned the medicine of hugging really works."

Without words. 'Be still and know that I am God.' . . . No matter how important our words are after the experience, the important things in life are communicated without words. At times of birth or death or discovery of love, what words are of any use, really? At the marathon, much was communicated between strangers by the simple experiment of touching each other's faces without words. Be still and know who I am, and be known."

I can touch my own body. "The poundage is the same but I can and really should get more support from my body. I can touch my own body and nothing says no one else can't touch me. Those weights are still there but last night I literally could feel strength come into me when I at last let others touch me."

Right on. "To experience sensuous feelings as a gift—unashamedly and without guilt in the presence of God, is a breakthrough."

"I can just imagine Jesus hugging and loving his followers."

"It seems as if he knew how bound up we all are! And by giving himself he was able to give to us through the centuries how great is our bodily love—to really live it—to melt together—our spiritual, physical, intellectual, and emotional existence."

"We need to be further nurtured and reshaped by other

communities of persons who have learned to love as God loves—freely, forgivingly, steadfastly, unconditionally, in deed (feeding, clothing, touching, holding, etc.)."

"The Puritan ethic that says feelings are not allowed, or less than human—the feelings of fear, pain, anger, and sexuality—has pervaded our whole culture—love is the only allowed feeling and no one seems to remember what that is."

"Christianity is love to me now, after Kirkridge, but now it is something to be experienced; through acceptance; freedom to relate to others through touch, caring, and support."

"Touching a fellow human being in 'love' is like reaching out and touching God's community and God."

Sex-body-touch. **"For the first time, I feel bubbly and my body tingles to the tips with a strength. There is a sense of being integrated into the whole universe—a sense of oneness, a flowing of endless warmth and lightheartedness."**

"In the smile, the touch, the sound of each person—each day—each act of love and understanding—but even more in the cries for help I will hear, will I find Christ because he lives in me?"

"God is love—and I've experienced it here to the soles of my feet—to the depth of my womb—to the tips of my fingers—to the warmth of my heart—and to the reservoir of my soul."

"I've been (and feel no guilt either on this score) learning to feel my emotions as a woman. Doris washed my dirty me with her tears and dried me with her hair."

SUGGESTIONS

Peak Experience and Continuing Meaning

Maslow's notion of "peak experiences" is an important ingredient in the Shalom approach. It is assumed that all the participants are capable of "peaking" if they will relax their inhibitions, overcome their middle-class propensity to see meaning in rational, ideational terms alone, and open themselves in sensitivity to themselves (including their own bodies and physical drives) and to others. There is an aspect of meaning which may not be sufficiently developed by Maslow, however, and that is the persistence and continuity of meaning. That which does not last is not meaningful, though it may be intense at the moment. More attention ought to be given toward the end of the retreat to discuss ways in which the experiences and insights from the retreat can be applied to situations and problems at home.

Meaning is enabled to persist in at least three ways: (1) by a change in the being of the experiencer, so that the way in which he now relates to reality and copes is fundamentally changed by the experience; (2) by a repetition of the original meaning experience; and (3) by a conceptualization of the original experience so that its implications can be applied in a variety of situations. The first way is favored by Maslow and is, ideally, what Shalom is trying to do. However, because of the brevity of the encounter and the fact that the group is so vitally involved in the process of self-discovery (a group which is unique to one weekend, so that the process of social reinforcement cannot be expected to continue), makes it questionable to expect the reconstitution of the self to be thorough enough to endure. What will persist is warm memories of the Kirkridge experience but those are not sufficient. The second approach was taken by the churches based on the revivals. The revival provided the peak experience, the weekly worship became a means of recelebrating that original experience and keeping it current. This is the pattern followed by the "repeaters," those who return to relive the original experience in the familiar surroundings. Most of the participants seemed to find it difficult to imagine that this experience could be reproduced in their own local church ("I know the church back home; these methods would never work") which would seem to indicate that a straightforward repetition of the experience on the local level is not a real possibility. Therefore some other way must be found to preserve the meaning. The third approach, conceptualization, may be somewhat antagonistic to the Human Potential Movement in its present phase. However, if meaning is to endure, it is almost inevitable that more structured reflection on experience will have to take place. The process out of which these theological reflections came is a helpful beginning, but I suspect that more direction will have to be given in the development of the conceptualization of the experience, if it is to become a working philosophy which the participants can continue to develop and utilize in their own situations.

Right on! We hope as a result of a Shalom experience that the retreatant will experience a change, so that the way in which he now relates to reality and copes is fundamentally changed by the experience. Nothing keeps us from this high hope. And in some cases we have real evidence that this has occurred. But Runyon is also correct in saying that with the present lack of continued social reinforcement there is undoubtedly a real erosion of the experience. So we must pay attention to both the second and the third ways whereby meaning is enabled to persist.

We are much interested in the local church and the means whereby churches harness something of the power of the Human Potential Movement and make use of it in community building and in understanding and celebrating the Judeo-Christian story. Suffice here to say that we are dealing with a vast complexity and right now though we have some signs that something is possible there, a bridge must be built. We do not yet know how to bring it about. But we are determined to find the ways whereby it may be done. Our future research will be centered in this area.

As for the third approach, conceptualization, in some deep sense this has gone on with the retreatants, though we are determined to do a more thorough job in this area.

Social Implications

The social-and-political-problems dimension of life is almost totally absent from the theological reflections, which is the more surprising because the participants seem to be drawn largely from a fairly liberal theological orientation. Evidently no time is spent on the potential inherent in these methods for conflict resolution. One participant (the exception) agonized, "Gotta find some way to relate this to social evils—some way in addition to turning people on with love. Gotta get this into a political and economic shape. Don't feel that changing 'one by one' is enough. . . . How to feel it into the guts of public structures as well as individuals." You might feel hesitant to turn this discussion to these issues because it turns the focus away from the group itself, and would tend to divide the group in terms of political stances. Yet that is the real world, and if the Human Potential Movement is not able to free up persons to deal with it, its contribution is no more than that of the church which majors in giving persons good feelings and warm fellowship but hesitates to disturb them by raising any controversial issues.

Runyon has raised a critical and fiercely important issue and one that will not easily down. Elisabeth and I are deeply concerned about unjust structures. We called our retreat "Shalom" because we wanted to tie in to the biblical vision of what God intends for his world. It is not enough, we believe, for the lion and the lamb to lie down together in your belly. God intends that goodness and that peace for the whole creation. Our retreats because of their brevity, were aimed entirely at personal self-actualization. Thus we are now in a position to ask whether there is some correlation between this kind of personal experiencing and the suffering (unjust structures) of the world. We think we have some affirmative data here.

In our follow-up questionnaire, we asked, "Do you consider yourself more sensitive to the needs of the world?" Here is what some said:

> "At one time I thought that social and political action would help make this world a better place. Now I am pessimistic about the future of our civilization but more hopeful about the future of mankind. I see individuals as growing in love and understanding. Let society then go where it may."
>
> "I am more sensitive especially to the unhappiness and distress of others. I hold back less and am more apt to make the first verbal move."
>
> "Our retreat was one of many significant 'explosions' which are freeing me to turn from my internal inhibitions to needs of those around me."
>
> "While I always felt sensitive to the needs and problems of the world, I feel now that I understand them much better—also that I feel the pain of the world more now."
>
> "I think the retreat experience gave me an indication of what a fully human life could be like. With this in mind, it is easier to comprehend the devastation of people who for personal, economic, or political reasons are denied good relationships."
>
> "Before the retreat I was so wrapped up in the death of the nation, society, and the world that I was dying myself. When I would look in the mirror I was surprised to see that I looked as alive as I did because I felt so dead inside. Through the retreat I came to love myself, accept myself as a separate, free, and important person and have the joy of being loved by others and thus see more clearly the anger, hurt, and fear of people around me and also their need to be loved, seen, and understood.

While I still think the world is moving in the direction of death, I have some sense of resurrection and more importantly I care about people individually where they are. I think I have a more balanced understanding of the problems of people as they relate to society and vice versa. I think I can see solutions to problems and where I stand in the solution—a solution other than blowing up everything."

"The answer is yes if 'world' is translated into persons and feelings and needs with which they confront any situation. For example, I'm less interested in dealing with social issues on the level of information and education and instead think we have to deal with the fears, etc., which control our acceptance and use of information."

"Being less concerned with myself and my problems, I could be more aware and concerned with the needs and problems of the world."

The following table shows what percentage of people in the Kirkridge and LaForet Groups felt they had become more sensitive to the needs of the world. A content analysis revealed that many persons had interpreted the question in terms of persons' needs rather than in terms of social issues. The second table shows clearer differences between the two groups.

Sensitivity to World's Needs
Comparison Between Kirkridge and LaForet Groups

	Kirkridge		LaForet	
	%	No.	%	No.
No answer	2.9	3		
As sensitive as before	7.6	8	12.9	4
No change	25.7	27	16.1	5
More sensitive	63.8	67	71	22
	100.0	105	100.0	31

World's Needs—Social Issues
Versus Needs of Persons
Comparison Between Kirkridge and LaForet Groups

	Kirkridge		LaForet	
	%	No.	%	No.
Needs of persons	80.6	13	45.5	10
Social issues	19.4	54	54.5	12
	100.0	67	100.0	22

In this chart we see a significant difference between those persons with whom we worked at Kirkridge and those with whom we worked at LaForet. At LaForet we worked with persons for eleven days. During the first three days of the experience the Shalom Retreat method was used to build intense community. We called the communities house churches. After the community was built we engaged in a sociodrama (a Black Power take-over of the camp) which lasted six more days. We thereafter spent two days in conceptualizing the experience. In this instance the wholeness of the Christian gospel was taken into account in interpersonal relations and in regard to unjust structures. Thus we note here a significant difference in changed world orientation.

Our understanding of the nature of the Christian religion lays an imperative upon those who seek to follow that way to love themselves, each other, and the world. Thus we are committed to find the ways whereby the Shalom Retreat methods may become as significant for turning people on to the world in the same way that the methods "turn on" persons to others and themselves.

The implication that "the Shalom Retreat methods' contribution is no more than that of the local church which majors in giving persons good feeling and warm fellowship but hesitates to disturb them by raising any controversial issues," is sufficiently close to cause discomfort but there is a striking difference in that we have real evidence that persons by means of the Shalom process do change their perspective and their behavior.

Sectarianism

The temptation toward sectarianism is strong in any experience-based movement. A strong sense of in-group loyalty develops, along with a growing conviction that others cannot and will not understand this experience. "Hope for the future is in groups like ours." "I doubt whether 95 percent of present church people will allow themselves to risk sufficiently or be challenged." On the one hand, the assertion is made that churches will only be relevant as they become sensitivity oriented; on the other, there seems to be no possibility of them developing in this direction or, even if they were willing, there would not be sufficient leadership. ("There aren't enough Jerrys and Elisabeths to go around.") The result is a basic frustration about the church which is neither resolved or turned in a creative direction. Could more time be spent discussing the realities of the church situation and an effort made by the retreat community to project realistic goals in terms of which their influence can be effective?

The danger of sectarianism is very high indeed. The leaders of this research are not interested in promoting sectarianism, and this book is being written in the hopes that we will begin to build the bridge between this kind of Human Potential experiencing and the local church. Our hope is in a pluralistic local church, one that does not insist upon homogeneity and that will "allow" this kind of experiencing and this kind of witnessing to go on. The danger lies in both directions: the local church forbidding the experiencing and the witnessing; the possibly narrow witness on the part of the retreatants—"unless you go my route, you cannot be saved." I see no easy way around this problem; we will have to go through this impasse.

Tactile Communication

Some theoretical work needs to be done on both the advantages and limitations of sexual feelings as the agency for the communication of Christian love. The old question of eros and agape needs to be reopened, since eros is now more positively valued by Christian thought than it was at the time of Nygren's original discussion. It remains true, however, that the human embrace expresses not only warmth and support toward the other but also the need of the self to possess the other. Thus, there may be an ambiguity written into sexuality that makes it necessary for an interpretation to accompany the embrace so that the recipient will receive the right divine message, i.e., that this embrace signifies the love that frees, not the love that manipulates or possesses. (Of course, the person with masochistic or dependent tendencies may actually prefer the latter.)

For many persons not involved in the Human Potential Movement, the implied freedom of touching and embracing may cause the most fright and criticism. For those inside the movement a totally different perspective emerges. Bonhoeffer says, "We will not know what we do not do." We need both to

listen to Runyon's caveat and also to experiment with a deep sense of love.

A POSTSCRIPT: A THEOLOGICAL PERSPECTIVE FROM GERMANY

Frau Marlies Cremer has been for many years a member of the staff of the Bad Boll Evangelical Academy in West Germany. She is highly skilled both in sociology and theology. For three years she was a member of the Los Angeles Goals Project which raised and sought to answer the question whether the religious community could significantly assist in the planning process of a great city. In 1970 she was in this country again for several months to learn more about what is going on in the Human Potential Movement and to learn to use some of its skills. During August 1970 she participated as a member of a Shalom Retreat. Thereafter I asked for her analysis:

Here are some of her comments concerning love:

> The participants experienced *love* in a new way. There is no more the deep gap between what in the churches is called love and love between man and woman.
>
> Love in the church often was experienced as some cool politeness and distant concern. Love in the church was often experienced as something humiliating to accept. The poor, the needy become objects of love—the others *gave* things and words to them without really knowing them.
>
> In the Shalom marathon people experienced that *love is a comprehensive event.* PEOPLE CANNOT LOVE WITH THEIR BRAINS AND WITH THEIR SENSE OF ETHICS ONLY. THEY ARE BEING DRAWN INTO THE DIMENSION OF LOVE AND TRUST. THEIR EMOTIONS ENTER INTO THIS NEW EXPERIENCE. They face unknown forces within themselves—they speak about their demons and about their own strength or love, it sounds like *libido and destrudo, Liebestrieb and Todesreb*—to speak in very simplified terms. The church has spoken about all this but never allowed people to face these forces within themselves—the white churches (not the black churches) together with modern society have put on ice the forces underneath the skin. Still these forces are at work within us. The Shalom marathon did the job of *unfreezing* these forces. Only by experiencing these forces is man able to make full use of them, to enjoy love and strength, to fight openly the destructive forces, or to challenge them in a way that they do no harm to living beings. Usually, when these forces all of a sudden are being set free, people become afraid of what is within them. Therefore the

analyst goes a long way step by step. In the Shalom marathon, methods were being applied which made it possible to do the unfreezing much faster.

This process became possible because mutual trust was built at the beginning. The persons experienced here the power of a loving and supporting congregation. Here to me is the point, where there was experienced: "God is Love, Love is God." People drew their understanding of love from the scriptures, they became aware, that they never had allowed themselves to experience fully, whether this love would carry them; they really had never "left the boat." Here we left the boat and were carried.

At this point, I think, the *experience of transcendence* comes in. It has another aspect also—people—especially Christians with an overdeveloped superego gave themselves freely without fear because it had been made clear, that the others are here to see to it that no harm is being done to their own growth and to their relationship to people who are near to them.

The freeing and at the same time frame-setting aspect of the scriptures came to bear here, we may say the freeing gospel and the helpfully frame-setting "law" in a broad sense. In simple words, the people knew that they would not be lost in their new freedom.

This "liberating but not license" is what I understand from what is written about love. Some sentences, for my feeling, are very enthusiastic. I think it was necessary for many to experience that enthusiasm has a place in the church. Paul takes this for granted, but he says that it is important to interpret the events of the spirit and to see what they do for the growth of the church and for the "common good." So he brings the enthusiastic experience in relation to reality; their impact on reality will prove whether they are valid. For my experience, the Shalom marathon *was* valid, very valid.

CHAPTER 8
Celebration

How do people celebrate if no one tells them how or what to do? This was one of our questions as we designed Shalom Retreats and planned our research design. The answer is very simple. If they have had a rich life together, they celebrate very well. They do natural, spontaneous things that act out how they feel. They do beautiful things.

By the last morning of the retreat, we are a community rich in significant relationships. Something has happened of great importance. We have moved past formality into a deep sense of involvement with one another. There is trust in process. We are ready to celebrate. Something has happened. Something is happening. Something will happen.

MINI-CELEBRATIONS

Of course there have been many mini-celebrations throughout the retreat. In fact, we celebrate each time after a person finishes working on the mat. Whether he has won some great victory or experienced only a minor breakthrough, the whole group affirms him and celebrates him. This is usually in the form of rock and roll. Here we focus upon and rejoice in a person. To be celebrated in this way recalls our experiences when we were children and celebrated our birthday. Love is expressed to each person in the form of physical affection and closeness.

Better let one of the retreatants tell it:

> I saw the talking and telling and sharing as the sermon. I saw the dealing with agony, the pain, the hurt, the suffering, the guilt, the anger as going through the fires of hell and it was absolute HELL for me. I was fighting for my life. Though willing hands and hearts were working like hell to pull me through, when it got down to the nitty-gritty, I was the one that had to deal with it and push and drag myself through all that crap. I was giving birth to me and the labor was hell.

I saw the rocking and rolling as a burial ceremony and, oh God, it was marvelous to not exist. It was marvelous to be dead.

I saw the hugging as the resurrection and it was marvelous to rise again a new person and to be welcomed into all that waiting love, to be cleaned up by the tears, to be anointed with that soothing oil. Sue washed me in tears, anointed me with her love, and she dried my tears with her hair. I felt I knew what Jesus felt like with Mary Magdalene. And *giving*—I did not feel they left me ever after that. They gave me what I needed as long as I needed it and they will always give it to me. I am a human being and I have a vision of what heights it can reach. There is always more. I want more!

Feedback is also a time when many mini-celebrations occur. As a matter of fact when the formal feedback occurs, each person in the most real sense is celebrated as he or she receives the feedback. The feedback is given, both negative and positive, in love and at the same time there is much good humor and laughter, and sometimes tears. And in the laughter and tears and in the remembering there is real celebration.

THE CLOSING CELEBRATION

This closing celebration has already been briefly described in chapter 3. It is planned to occur immediately before the closing meal and the end of the retreat. While the retreatants are writing their theological reflections, we make the simple preparations for the celebration. We place a jug of wine and a loaf of bread on a flat board on the mat. Grape juice is there for those who do not drink wine.

When the theological reflections are finished and everyone has returned to "the pit," we say: "We have had a beautiful time together. It's time to celebrate. The bread and wine are here; hymnbooks and some Bibles are on the mat; and we are here. The celebration has no leader. We are all leaders. Let us do whatever will rightfully express our feeling."

The Celebration Is Not a Ritual

Thomas Harris defines ritual in an interesting fashion.

> A ritual is a socially programmed use of time where everybody agrees to do the same thing. It is safe, there is no commitment to or involvement with another person, the outcome is predictable and it can be pleasant insofar as you are "in step" or doing the right thing. There are worship rituals, greetings rituals, cocktail party rituals, bedroom rituals. The ritual is designed to

get a group of people through the hour without having to get close to anyone. They may, but they don't have to. It is more comfortable to go to a High Church Mass than to attend a revival service where one may be asked, "Are you saved, brother?" Sexual relations are less awkward in the dark for people for whom physical intimacy has no involvement at the level of personality. There is less chance for involvement in throwing a cocktail party than in having a dinner for six. There is little commitment, therefore little fulfillment. Rituals, like withdrawal, can keep us apart.[1]

Celebration is the opposite of ritual. Here is deep personal involvement, commitment and unpredictability. It is designed for a happening to occur; it is designed for warmth and intimacy.

How It Begins

The celebration begins in many different ways. Sometimes we simply sit there in silence. But it is not an empty silence or a nervous silence. It is fraught with meaning and feeling. We "know" each other, we care deeply about each other, we have been through it together; something will happen. "Don't push the river, it flows by itself." And something does happen.

Sometimes we begin with a quiet discussion of whatever comes up. The mood, though, is not philosophic, but celebrative. We are probably remembering and gently struggling with meaning.

Sometimes people two by two or in small groups will begin to talk with one another. There's no one to tell us what to do. We just do it.

But usually the bread and the wine become the focus of attention. We just sit and look at them. Some are undoubtedly struggling with the meaning of these simple elements; others may be wondering who will pour the wine and then break the bread.

Once somebody noticed that the cork was still in the bottle and then there ensued a long discussion of what it means to be uncorked. When the cork was finally removed with a loud pop, we celebrated our uncorked condition.

Oftentimes someone just moves forward on his own initiative and pours some wine for himself or for another. And

---

[1]Thomas A. Harris, *I'm Ok: You're Ok* (New York: Harper & Row, 1969), p. 116.

so it begins. On still another occasion the group decided that they wanted a very special person to "do the honors." He had had a deep sense of "I'm no good" and had opened what he deemed his life of failure to us all. He had found real joy. They wanted the bread and wine from him.

The Moods

1. Something different happens each time because the group is different. Sometimes the group is very quiet, speaking quietly together and by twos or in small clusters; sometimes the group is very noisy; most of the time there is a combination of the two.

2. Spontaneity is an essential characteristic of all of the celebrations. Different leaders emerge at different times and the group may swiftly move from one mood to the other.

3. Joy is apparent usually in everybody. Something beautiful has happened and we have all been a part of the drama. Strangers have become friends. Victories have been won and vows have been made. Our humanness has been exposed, we are unashamedly human; we rejoice in our bodies and celebrate the unity of body and spirit. Affection flows easily and naturally. We are glad.

What Are the Essential Components?

1. *The celebration emerges out of a rich life together.* It is not imposed from above (there is no Big Daddy to tell us what to do, when to stand and when to sit, when to sing and when to pray, when to begin and when to end). It emerges from the deeps of our life together. This is a critical dimension of real celebration. Something is; something has happened; something is happening; something will happen.

2. Since no one decides for the others what will be done, *the celebration is a happening in the deepest sense of the term.* It is people centered and people directed. Anyone is free to contribute to the celebration and anyone is free to lead.

Some things seem to happen at every celebration.

1. *It is a highly personal time.* People who have met in some deep sense find some time to be together to celebrate meanings. No formal words of communion are spoken (for we recognize that for some there the bread and the wine may be nothing more than ancient symbols of celebration), but we

have frequently noted that one person will go to another and as he gives the bread and/or the wine he may say the words, "This is my body, this is my blood." Or they may simply without speaking give to each other the bread and the wine. In each retreat these beautiful and tender moments have occurred.

A great moment occurred for me during our retreat with Albright College students. After the wine had been poured, I said, "If there is a Jew present, it would be especially meaningful to me to receive the wine from him or her." Suddenly four young men were before me. One of them said, "I guess we ought to say a prayer first." And so they did, in Hebrew—a prayer from their own rich heritage—and then they put the wine to my lips. When we hugged each other, ancient meanings came alive for me and for them as well.

2. *There is always singing.* Hymnbooks with many of the old favorite songs are easily available and songs are available that are new. Usually it is not the old hymns which are sung but the new ones. Occasionally I will suggest one that has special meaning to me but otherwise we sing songs such as "They Will Know We Are Christians by Our Love," "Joy Is Like the Rain," and "Lord of the Dance."

Some groups do great singing, others do not.

3. *Usually there is some form of dancing.* But this dancing is essentially characterized by spontaneity. Once a retreatant over sixty began to dance. She had come to the retreat tense, drawn, and worried but she had found love and affirmation and new strength. When she began spontaneously to dance we all knew that a really beautiful thing was happening. She danced the Charleston and other dances much alive in the twenties. It was a deeply religious dance that helped us to celebrate her and rejoice in her. She gave us a gift none of us will forget.

All kinds of dancing emerge. The song "Lord of the Dance" often gets us to our feet and as a group doing innovative dancing. When the spirit is turned on, the body inevitably is involved, it has to move, too. On a number of retreats the singing of "When the Saints Come Marching In" gets us all into spontaneous dancing.

Sometimes unusual things happen.

1. Oftentimes toasts are drunk to members of the group.

"To John, who cut the longest umbilical cord in history." "To Barbara, who is no longer a rock."

2. Once a young minister who had at first impressed everyone as really successful, really a winner, the kind of person who is usually in charge, threw himself down upon the mattress at the beginning of the celebration, saying, "I've nothing to offer you right now but my weakness."

3. Once we gathered around a couple whom we all loved but whose problems still seemed immense. We gathered in a tight human ball around them and simply groaned.

4. Once we played a game of chucklebelly, a game we played as children. Each person puts his head on the belly of someone else, an interlocking chain of people, and then someone begins to laugh. It is quite amazing the wonderful good feelings which emerge. If an outsider had come in, he would have thought us demented. It was hilariously celebrative.

5. Looking into each other's eyes. On the first evening strangers looked into each other's eyes during the first nonverbal. Now friends look into each other's eyes with new meanings, a real celebration.

6. On the first evening of a retreat one of our retreatants during the second nonverbal cried out, "Don't touch me," and she disengaged herself from the group and sat alone. During the course of the retreat she found the healing in the hands of people who cared and found great strength and new courage. During the course of the celebration she came to me saying, "You have a full cup, pour it on me." I looked at her beautiful hair and clean white blouse and said, "You can have it all, take it and drink." But she insisted, "I want you to pour your wine on me." I knew she meant it and I did. Then she called for others to pour their wine on her too. She was soaked with wine and ecstatic. Later she said that she wanted to take the experience in through her skin.

Some things do not happen. We place hymnbooks, old and new, on the mat before the celebration begins. We put some Bibles there, too. Only occasionally has someone chosen to read from the Bible and only one person (besides the Jewish students) has freely offered to pray. And no one has yet preached a sermon.

Traditional hymns, verbal prayer, and sermons, all seem

noticeable by their absence. What this means is highly conjectural. This question is not a putdown of traditional hymns. Many of us are still deeply moved by them or by verbal prayer or sermons, but we need to ponder this evidence. Could it be that vocal prayer, Bible reading, hymns, and sermons have become so unreal and hollow that introducing them in the presence of the deep and genuine feelings which have been evoked seems almost sacrilegious. There may be important implications here for the worship of the future.

Ecstasy

One of the strong themes which runs through the theological reflections is that of ecstasy. It weaves in and out of the writings like a gay, sparkling brook making its way down a mountainside, sparkling in the sunshine, passing through the shady glen, disappearing for awhile and then reemerging with impish gaiety. Ecstasy is an important aspect of the celebration experience.

Ecstasy means literally the state of being outside oneself. It is a state accompanied by joy, enthusiasm, and a sense of the transcendent. That is, there exists as an integral part of the ecstatic experience the feeling that one is a part of a moving reality that is greater than the self. The metaphor, "He was beside himself with joy" is another way of saying he was ecstatic.

Though most of our church experiences are now devoid of the ecstatic experience, our history is replete with witnesses to the ecstatic experience: the ecstatic visions of prophets and psalmists, religious dances, the ecstatic behavior of King David home from battle. The birthday of the church, Pentecost, was an ecstatic experience for all those early disciples who "were all together in one place (Acts 2:1)." The people who saw them said, "These people have to be drunk. Nobody could feel that good without being drunk (Jud version)." Peter in his great sermon that day had to deny the charge, saying, "Men of Judea and all who dwell in Jerusalem, let this be known to you, and give ear to my words. For these men are not drunk, as you suppose, since it is only the third hour of the day (Acts 2:14-15)."

We remember, too, the beautiful story of a blind man Jesus healed who "entered the Temple, leaping and praising God";

the ecstasy of poets, Quakers, revivalists. Each of us has probably some memory of great ecstasy to which the transcendent is related.

And here are contemporary ecstatic utterances emerging from the midst of a Shalom Retreat.

Profuse imagery. "I see a tree with all her leaves shivering with a calm excitement because they know they are wanted, they are allowed to shiver and dance or even let go if they want. A rippling flow of feeling, pouring its juices on every inch of my body and soaking into my soul. Now I'm able to weep without trying to weep; laugh without trying to laugh; dancing without trying to dance. I love you with an excited calm. Yes, rolling in clover, embraced with someone who cares, just for fun. Let's go to a movie! Let's make love! Let's make joy! Let's make peace! Let's just make! Not in compulsion or oughtness. But in just letting the 'making' flow out and over and under and through. On and on it goes. Infinite. And I can feel the sheer delight of a cool water caress my body—both inside and out."

"I am a bird with my wings stretched out—just soaring through the clouds—feeling the warmth of the sun—hugging my tired body. It's moving again. I have so much to share. And I don't have to force it anymore. Like reading theology or the Bible or whatever else hits my desk. I may just hug the book because there is a small sentence in it that grabs hold and that's all. Just being myself and letting it happen from that affirmation."

Music. "The bells are ringing, resonating with the sounds of the universe. There are new sounds for me along with the familiar. It's a new orchestration and I am pausing to listen. Some of the sounds are louder, more familiar; others are new, distant but I hear them drawing closer."

Identity. "I am Mary! Hurrah!"

Beyond words and ideas. "Easy does it! Joy flowing through people and allowing everybody to be—with no because. Hold your body closely and loosely in tender strength. I see a bird soaring through the sky wounded, imperfect with some of her feathers damaged and hurt. But oh, how beautiful to realize that I am that bird, too, and so are we all. I still don't know how to define this in categories or theories or theology and I really don't care to define it in this way at all—so I won't."

"*Surprise!* Because I did not want to come to this retreat I came so empty thinking I did not want or need. But how wrong I was. I know now that God really loves me and that I love Him and that it is really unconditional. I had been told that before and did not really believe it. Wow! Do I ever now!"

"I used to feel I had to always ask for his forgiveness; that gets very trying but I know he loves me and forgives me anyway. He is a spirit of power that is sometimes hard to believe but has showed his face to me here. The sadness I feel for the world just kills me. I want to shake it and say, "Wake up! There's so much more, more, MORE!"

A new day dawning. "How can mere words, when I'm learning how much more feelings mean, describe what this has meant to a marriage that was faltering, and a woman who was failing just about everything, describe the feelings about this experience.

"The old words seem mundane and empty in comparison unless the new connotations which I have learned are applied. When I look in my husband's face I see joy and it's not a *ride* or a *detergent* or a wishy-washy palliative, but a living wonder that makes life suddenly beautiful, meaningful, and happily contemplated. That's great after the fear of the future I had before."

From a retreat in December. "The wind is blowing just now through the trees at the top of this mountain and it echoes a thought that has come and gone in my mind these past few days: 'The wind blows where it wills, and you hear the sound of it, but you do not know from where it comes or where it is going; so it is with everyone who is born of the Spirit.'

"How could one know that help would come from an unexpected direction, that tears would come and liberate one from the knots tied inside—knots made up of old images and constraints? Still constraints are here, I feel them—but it is somewhat like the old Sarah story—the barren one shall give birth, long past the hour when birth was thought possible.

"I dreamed last night of a new apartment—in surroundings that were a combination of the old Chinese embassy where I live and the great hotels of Miami Beach. A friend had some things which just fit it perfectly—although she is Jewish—a Christmas tree, a small fir from the woods, a lovely, fragrant, perfect one—and after some of our friends carried it in and we had it all decorated, I realized that there was no room for any of my things—furniture wouldn't fit here. I was afraid; what a foolish mistake, Anne! You really had no forethought—but then this morning, talking about it, all that it conveys is good news—the old baggage is really not so necessary; I can let it go, because the Christmas child is being born. Halleluia!

"The dance of life, new life, begins for me around the green tree."

The Polarity of Joy and Pain

It is our belief that the great expression of joy in the midst of celebration at the retreat is closely related to the experiencing of pain. Pain is the fire that hollows out the cup that holds the rich wine of joy. Prior to the retreat many were hiding from pain, their own and that of others close around them; they had shut themselves out from the pain of the world. All of us in some sense do this, some more than others. But it is not possible to participate in the retreat without being called to open one's heart to the pain of others and thereby get in touch with one's own pain. In the course of the retreat we find that the pain is bearable and that when pain is shared and when pain is received, there is another great experience awaiting us —on the other side joy awaits us.

O joy that seekest me through pain.
I do not ask to fly from thee.
I lay in dust life's glory dead
And from the ground there blossoms red
Life that shall endless be.[2]

Most of the retreatants experience this truth. Some verbalize it:

New focus. "I got a new focus to the biblical story. To choose to live the life of love, the life of the Christian, is to choose misunderstanding, sorrow, pain and rejection—the way of Jesus and the cross. Joy is there too—but it's harder to find. I feel many Christians do not find it; they are solemn, down, pained—and call such a stance righteousness. In fact, there is more joy in a bar-room than in a Christian gathering, even the holy feast. No wonder the world is slow to 'bug in.' Many of us carry the pain of the world so tied to us, we become pain.

---

[2]George Matheson, "O Love That Wilt Not Let Me Go."

"The depth of the hurt and fear and anger in people is deep and all pervading. There's no room or hope for equally deep and pervading joy apart from a loving, supporting community. The pain can be found alone. The joy cannot. Hence the church. We need the church for our very life. Apart from it, we become angry, burdened, and walled off from people."

We need others. "This retreat has taught me that a man's Christianity (or sharing with Christ, symbol of love transcendent over pain) is not a thing for him alone. It needs others to exist. Without them it becomes pain transcendent.

"This experience has given me hope that my faith as a Christian can become sweet and gentle and part of others and I will cease to feel it as angry, tragic sense of alienation from the rest of the world I know and love."

Empathy. "I have seen enacted in the marathon something of what it means to lay down one's life for another in terms of the total presentness of person to person. I experience this. I also experience that the feeling of one person—be it pain or joy—causes me to touch the same emotion in myself which means that we both suffer, both are healed, both celebrate."

What They Said Months Later

In the questionnaire sent to our retreatants (four to ten months after the retreat) we asked, "What significance did the celebration at the retreat have for you personally?" Most of the respondents answered the question and almost all the responses were very favorable.

Among almost one hundred replies, there *were six negative comments.* All the rest were favorable.

Negative comments. "It left me a little sick—especially the communion where the name of Jesus Christ was not formally mentioned."

"I feel that when taking communion I like more guilt and meditation, with the celebration coming afterwards in encounter."

"No great significance. It was warm and friendly."

"Little significance of which I am aware."

"Not too much significance of which I am aware."

"Not too much significance."

"Very little; my emotional state at that time was not conducive to celebration."

Illustrations of positive comments. "I was motivated to begin a new life style."

"Became aware of what celebration means, for the first time."

"Demonstrated that the 'church' could be anywhere—anything—that it didn't have to be with mold on it—that it could be free and joyful."

"It dramatized the gulf between the formal, set, stiff ritual and a free, spontaneous human experience."

"I feel it enabled me to express where it was and what was happening to me. I had something to celebrate and people I felt I could celebrate with. It lingers in my being as 'authentic worship.'"

"I consider it my first communion—experienced tremendous feelings of joy and love and excitement."

"Never has worship (celebration) been so meaningful. I felt very close and loving toward those involved and very thankful to God for life and all that it can mean."

"It felt so free, liberating, joyous, genuine. It helped me to see worship as celebration and as releasing what has happened rather than creating and producing an experience of worship."

"I felt it was a pentecostal event which confirmed me in Christian spirit."

"Possibly for the first time I understood at a feeling level that you can trust people to be spontaneous."

"It was a weird experience to realize that you didn't have to be phony but I had been used to the old for over forty years and wasn't sure of the new but how glorious to be free for the first time to be who I am."

"It lifted me above the mire of problems of us all; it gave me a marvelous sense of group joy! It connected the historic experience with a 'now' event."

"It was probably the greatest feeling of sheer joy I have ever experienced; yet I don't feel it can be duplicated apart from the previous experience."

"It helped me to realize that I can react spontaneously in unstructured worship situation, without falling apart."

"I will never forget it. The Holy Spirit was just dripping. I felt a real sense of rededication and a joy that was really full."

"A terrific sense of joy and thankfulness—a rekindling of my relationship with God. I have never been in a group before where the 'oneness of man and God' was more clearly in evidence."

"We were all one. I had a feeling of being high in the true meaning of the word high. The one loaf and one bottle and lack of formality made this communion one of the most joyful experiences of my life."

"It has become the second most important time in my life. The dance I danced was my expression of utter joy. It was an ultimate act of praise to the Lord."

"The feeling comes back and overwhelms me with joy. A Minerva experience."

"It put my entire retreat into focus. Absolutely necessary to bridge retreat and return to the world. Gave my beliefs life. Recognition that man can only do so much for himself. First time I've felt 'Christian joy.'"

"The rituals of worship with which I was raised were/are most unsatisfactory. I have no words for the Shalom experience that would not be pretentious."

Something to Ponder

These strong positive comments made months after an experience of celebration should make us thoughtful—especially since the celebration they are talking about was one that was totally unplanned and without designated leaders. It was not structured within narrow "religious" parameters, and yet people saw in it vast religious significance. It is important to look at the principles operative here:

1. The deep level of celebration is possible because something has happened already. Thus the celebration arises from the life of the group and is not imposed upon the group.

2. The celebration itself is a happening. It is not planned; it happens. No one knows ahead of time what will be said or what will be done. The materials (instruments) of celebration are there, but whether they will be used or not, no one knows. The essential component of the celebration is the people who are there and what has already happened, is happening to them.

3. There is a high level of trust in process.

4. The leaders do not hold a tight rein. Preparation is made—it is they who put the jug of wine and loaf of bread on the mat. It is they who say, "Let's celebrate" but from then on they give up control.

5. Everyone feels entitled to contribute without feeling that he is intruding on leadership or assuming control. Each person does not of necessity take a turn at leading, but each is free to.

6. The group uses its own symbolic language and actions which have emerged from its own life of interaction.

7. Unexpected things happen. Unexpected things are expected to happen, but they are unplanned.

8. The celebration is characterized by unself-conscious participation. The group has a kind of organismic existence, with the predominant moods of joy and spontaneity.

Though the authors do not presume that we can easily transfer the Shalom celebration to the Sunday morning church service, we nevertheless hope that church worship leaders may learn something from our experience and be encouraged to trust the people more and take more risks.

CHAPTER 9

Policy Implications

The purpose of this chapter is to look again at each of the five major hypotheses concerning the study, review our findings, and point to policy implications of the data.

There are important implications for the church in the data which this study has produced. It is our hope that those who make policy on every level of the church's life, make decisions about financial expenditures, decide on what kind of education shall not be given under the auspices of the church, provide sanctions for experimentation and risk, encourage or discourage the updating of the church's life—that these policy-makers will pay attention to this research.

I. THE CHURCH AND THE ART OF LOVING

Hypothesis. By blending the Christian concept of the nature of love and the Human Potential methodologies, we can initiate significant behavior change in people.

Result. We have amply demonstrated that such behavior change was initiated and that long after the retreat (from four to ten months) the person, a significant other, and data from the FIRO-B test indicate behavior change in over 90 percent of the retreatants. This change was in a person's self-perception, in the way he expresses his feelings, and how he relates to his fellow man. If on a three-day retreat such significant help can be given people, how much greater opportunity does the church have—standing in continuous relation to its people—to train in the art of loving?

The church has both a beautiful vision of what man may become and a realistic appraisal of what he is. It has the means to help people get in touch with their power and to grow in the art of giving and receiving love. But most of its old methods are not working very well today. We are much too lost in rhetoric, lost in words. And this is dangerous. Sam Keen says it:

> Theology is a dangerous business because it fosters the illusion that there is some necessary connection between talk about God and the experience of the sacred. Any institution that has the audacity to speak in theological language has the obligation to keep its experience close to its rhetoric.[1]

Much of the talk that now goes on in the church is devoid of meaning and has little more effect than the coming and going of a fog because the experiences which ought to undergird the words and give them context are missing from church life.

The church holds up a high ideal of marriage and the family, but skill training for that life is almost totally missing from the church's ministry. It holds up the high ideal of loving your neighbor but does not show us how. It teaches us to love our enemies but gives us no skill training in enemy-love. It teaches "love your neighbor as yourself" but who ever heard of a church course offered on the skills of self-love? It teaches us to be good stewards of the earth, but is the church giving skill-training in loving the world while our rivers are being turned into sewers, our oceans polluted, and the very air we breathe fouled?

A very young minister once gave a sermon in a run-down mission in the innercity. A group of derelicts more hungry for soup than the Word of God listened drowsily for him to finish. He did finish, with a rousing rendition of "If" by Kipling: "If you can keep your head while all about you are losing theirs and blaming it on you, if you can trust yourself when all men doubt you . . . then you'll be a man, my son." A little old man way in the back of the room rose in his place and said, "Yeah, Reverend, but what if you can't?" And there's the rub. What if you can't? All the sermons in the world, telling us how we should behave, how we should love God, love ourselves, love man, love the world may only make us feel guilty because we can't. We need training in order to fulfill the high vision.

While no techniques can produce love, or even the intent to love, we now know methods that help remove the barriers to

---

[1]Sam Keen, *To a Dancing God* (New York: Harper & Row, 1970), p. 158.

giving and receiving love, that build trust, that help a person understand himself, to value himself and acquire skills in doing what he intends. Church leaders should know these methods and become proficient in their use.

In a society where many people are discouraged from trying to live up to their potential, it is important for the church to free individuals to dare face their needs, to experience their true feelings and develop their potentialities. Herbert Otto says:

> William James once estimated that the healthy human being is functioning at less than 10 percent of his capacity. It took more than half a century before this idea found acceptance among a small proportion of behavioral scientists. . . . Today, many well-known scientists such as Abraham Maslow, Margaret Mead, Gardner Murphy, O. Spurgeon English, and Carl Rogers subscribe to the hypothesis that man is using a very small fraction of his capacities. Margaret Mead quotes a 6 percent figure and my own estimate is 5 percent or less.[2]

But again it does little good to read, "When I look at thy heavens, the work of thy fingers, the moon and the stars which thou hast established: what is man that thou art mindful of him, and the son of man that thou dost care for him? Yet thou hast made him little less than God, and dost crown him with glory and honor (Ps. 8:4-6)" if the man dare not risk relationships because of rejection, if wanting to love and be loved he constantly falls on his face and grows more lonely all the time. Man *is* potential. We believe that he is capable of growing infinitely in his powers of giving and receiving love and of entering more and more deeply into life. But that potentiality needs to be tapped; he needs help—help the church can give if it will quit relying simply on its holy words and begin helping man find the skills he needs.

The church tends to concentrate on the sick to the neglect of those who are functioning reasonably well, "coping." *We do not discourage that good and loving gaze and the related actions; but we want to call attention also to the fact that the millions who come to church, who seem to be functioning all right, need help they are not getting.* Many of these people, seemingly all right, are living lives of quiet desperation, of

---

[2] *Saturday Review*, December 20, 1969, p. 17. Copyright 1969 Saturday Review, Inc.

intense loneliness; they want more out of life than they are getting, and many do not know the next steps. They are not likely to go to a psychiatrist's office. *We think human potential methods used by the church, interpreted in terms of the gospel's understanding of love, can make a difference for this large number of people.*

Policy Implication: Sanctions need to be provided in the church system, and training should be given to religious leaders in preparation for carrying out this ministry of releasing the human potential.

II. COMMUNITY BUILDING

Hypothesis. The Human Potential method has important implications for community building in the local church.

Result. Let's take a look at what happened on the retreats.

At seven o'clock on Thursday evening, most of the people were total strangers to each other. Because of the simple methods used, they were no longer strangers when the evening was over. They made a covenant of confidentiality, to hold their personal revelations as sacred. The next day we became an intense community, expressing honest feelings, deeply in touch with fear, anger, and pain. But as each person offered himself in openness, there was someone there for him. It was not simply leaders who ministered: everyone became a minister to the other in need. Before the retreat was over, intense loving community had emerged—not because the pain and ugliness of life were denied but because they were faced openly and honestly and because people had trust in the covenanted community and—each according to his lights—the covenant God. Our research points to the intensity of this community experience.

What do we learn here:

1. The hunger to give and receive love is in us all. It simply needs to be uncovered, tapped.

2. People have gifts to love and to bring healing to others. Carl Rogers says:

> One of the most fascinating aspects of any intensive group experience is the manner in which a number of the group members show a natural and spontaneous capacity for dealing

in a helpful facilitative and therapeutic fashion with the pain and suffering of others.[3]

3. People are dying of thirst in a fresh water lake. With man's hunger to give and receive love, what a pity that anyone is lonely, or lives a life of feeling rejected! In the retreat we found that the hunger to give and receive love, even though denied, was very near the surface and in the atmosphere of the retreat came to full bloom.

4. Intensity of community is not time-bound. How often we heard people say when leaving the retreat, "It seems I have known you forever," "I know the people on this retreat better than anyone else I know and they know me better than anyone else."

5. Love can be intended, therefore community can be intended. On the retreats, people intended community and were amazed how ordinary looking (at first) people became more and more beautiful before their eyes.

6. Love (community) is a response to need, and as persons get in touch with their need to be loved, they find it flowing toward them, not held back, not doled out in small amounts but given, pressed down, shaken together, and running over.

7. Honest expression of feeling, and openness are powerful community-builders.

The small-group approach is imperative in the life of the church today. But most small groups have a fatal flaw: they plateau. A kind of gentlemen's agreement exists, never verbalized but fully understood in the group, "I won't threaten your 'status quo' if you won't threaten mine." The group finds a level of safety, a place of maximal risk and therefore minimal growth. In order for small groups to be groups to grow in, there must be a commitment to a method which keeps people risking openness and honesty, of idea and feeling, with each other; a method which builds trust and encourages the giving and receiving of love.

The commitment to method is *the contract.* If a group does not have a designed contract for growth, the contract for hiddenness and plateau is made by default. The chances for

---

[3] From Carl Rogers in *Challenges of Humanistic Psychology,* ed. James F. Bugental (New York: McGraw-Hill, 1967), p. 266. Copyright 1967 by McGraw-Hill, Inc. Used by permission of McGraw-Hill Book Company.

growth are few, and the chances for boredom and death are many.

Church groups should be based on love, and the operant aspects of love should be made plain: seeing, hearing, intending goodwill, needing, being there for each other, theological reflection, and celebration. In our churches there is too often the wearing of masks, nonhearing, the pose of needing nothing (independence and self-sufficiency), merely formal confession (no absolution, not empowering), with worship a ritual instead of a celebration. If growth is to be facilitated, the operant components of love must become explicit and be a part of the contractual life of churches and church groups.

The Protestant Reformation was built on the mutual ministry of all believers, but we have come a long way from that fundamental concept of the life of the church. We need to return again to that fountainhead of wisdom and affirmation. We really can be ministers to each other; we really can bring healing to one another; we can be there for each other without first having a lot of technical training. These Shalom Retreats give us every encouragement to believe that the mutual ministry of all believers is a right one. But it will not just happen—in the life of the church we have to set up the conditions within which this ministry can take place.

Part of mutual ministry is to be open to giving and receiving feedback. Previously in the life of the church we may have thought of it as judgment. We are not encouraging the recovery of the church as a judgmental community, a judgment that encourages the feeling "I'm not good." Rather we are encouraging the kind of community in which love is strong and trust is real enough to make it possible for the truth to be spoken in love. Because most of us as church members do not have the benefit of such feedback, our pilgrimage of faith is lonely; and because we have no one to challenge our plateaus and our misty flats, we stay there choosing safety, loneliness, and dullness instead of the excitement and joy of risk and growth.

Many times we see feedback in negative terms. On our retreats, however, we find that there is more positive feedback than negative, that far from people thinking of themselves more highly than they ought to think, most of us estimate ourselves and our potential in weak and lifeless terms compared with how we are viewed by others. So to open oneself to negative feedback is also to open oneself to really take in the strength and the goodwill of others as well. And that is life-giving.

The *house church* concept is now getting more and more popular as a means of living in and rejoicing in the kind of community we are describing here. The early church met chiefly in believers' homes, and that only partly because Christianity was outlawed. "House" implies familiness, warmth, intimacy, goodwill, love, a place where need is acknowledged openly and where confession is made, forgiveness and absolution received; where one may come to lick his wounds, rejoice (in who we are and who we hope to become) in his little and big victories—in brief, a place to be in the context of love and acceptance. It is a place from which to go with a sense of enablement and empowerment. House churches are now evident all over the country. Some are composed of those who find the present local church too sterile for them to endure; but because they want to take their pilgrimage of faith seriously, they have joined with like-minded souls in a house church. Others have a tenuous relationship to a local church, participating in it in a highly selective fashion. Yet others are an integral part of a local church. Such arrangements will undoubtedly continue, with variations, in the '70s.

We see house churches as an especially important vehicle for calling forth the kind of experiencing of love and the kind of growth we are talking about in this book. Hopefully they will both encourage and challenge the local church to pick up again the very tools which made Christianity a redemptive force in the world and a source of healing and power.

Policy Implication. The exploration and promotion of the house church concept as a means whereby the church may promote intensive group life and promote training in *the art of loving.* These may or may not be related to traditional local churches. Some may grow out of theological seminaries' lay education efforts.[4]

---

[4]This has happened already through New York Theological Seminary.

Two important references: a book by Philip A. Anderson and Arthur L. Foster is soon to be published on this subject. Two chapters of the book are published in the CTS Bulletin, December 1970. Another important report is to be found in *Survey,* a publication of the Presbyterian Church in the U.S., March 23, 1970.

III. INTENSIVE EXPERIENCES AND THE BIBLICAL STORY

Hypothesis. Intensive experiences utilizing Human Potential procedures can be understood in terms of the biblical story.

Result. In chapter 6 we have shown ample evidence that our retreatants readily understood their retreat experience in terms of the biblical story. This we consider good news for them, and potentially good news for the churches.

Sam Keen says:

> Until recent years the keystone of personal identity was participation in the shared stories, legends, and myths of a tribe, nation, cult or church. The past, present and future of the individual were bound together by the memories and hopes of a people to which he belonged. With the birth of secular, pluralistic technological society, a new type of man has emerged, the man without a story, the rootless, protean man living without the stability of a tradition which he remembers with pride or a future he waits with longing.[5] . . . Modern man has lost his way in the forest, he cannot light the fire or say the prayer, and he is dangerously close to losing his ability to see his life as part of any story.[6]

In our research we have demonstrated that for these people who shared the retreats with us, the story is still alive. Granted that most of those represented by our data came from churches and returned to churches, they are nevertheless modern man, too; yet the story is alive in them. They found this experience illumined by remembering Jesus, calling Lazarus from the grave; by demon exorcism; by the woman taken in adultery; the alabaster box, crucifixion, resurrection, and many other biblical stories and themes.

The church is a stream of history-making. It rejoices in its shared history with Judaism, and this Judeo-Christian stream is rich with life-guiding and life-fulfilling stories. One's individual, personal story in this context has rich meaning.

The Bible is a rich treasure of such stories. When it is imposed upon man in any age with narrowness and as a tight belief-system, it restricts and squashes life. Modern man is not likely to get or stay in that kind of box. I like to think of the history of the church (including the Bible) as an attic (the

---

[5] Keen, op. cit., p. 71.

[6] Ibid., p. 85.

church has never thrown anything away; it's all there, the glory and the shame). We are free to browse around in the attic, to repair and polish old pieces, to use old symbolisms, old stories to illumine our lives and give them meaning. Because we are a part of that stream of history-making, it is all ours, there for enriching the meaning of our lives.

The experience of the wilderness-wandering is an integral part of the biblical story. In this new time we are going through a wilderness experience in our history again; we are wandering around in a new wilderness. In many ways we have lost our direction. Many no longer believe in the God who goes before in "a cloud by day and a pillar of fire by night," no longer believe in the God of the prophets nor in him who said, "I have come that you might have life abundantly." But if this experience of the 1970's wilderness is set within the larger story of wilderness wanderings, it takes on new meaning, and a new hope arises that our wandering in the wilderness will cease, we will get our direction again. So the wilderness is endurable after all.

A peak-experience, Minerva experience, mountaintop experience—call it what you will—somehow gains an added dimension and a whole new set of meanings when it is seen not in isolation but within a long history of a pilgrim people who experienced the transcendent, who said, "God is. . . ," who said, "Let us build three tabernacles here," who saw a burning bush and heard the voice of the Lord, who could say, "In the year that King Uzziah died, I saw the Lord, high and lifted up and his train filled the temple."

That day is not gone. Modern man in this new age still experiences the transcendent, and the biblical story illumines his experiences in a wonderful way, pointing to unique depths of peace, joy, and hope.

The greatest treasure the church has is not its beautiful buildings or anything else it possesses; the great treasure is the long saga of a pilgrim people whose glory is that they are called and troubled and glorified by their disturbing belief in God. And now again, in our day of wilderness-wanderings, when many who are a part of that stream of history-making can no longer believe in God, when there is loss of confidence in the transcendent, the great treasure is the story, and the church has the responsibility of keeping that story alive.

The modern clergyman needs to fulfill two primary functions: (1) as one who understands process, he should know the various means of assisting a *person* on his pilgrimage without imposing a fixed map or someone else's journey. He should be able to assist *groups* in releasing their latent power and maximizing their potential. He should have skill to help persons in the group to minister to each other. In this role he can give assistance in personal pilgrimage, in calling forth community, and in giving training in the art of loving. (2) He must be a man who knows the story, who is turned on to its beauty, accepts its glory and its shame, and sees his own life illumined by it. He should be one who knows how to help persons mine the gold in the hills of that story, to make it their very own.

You will notice the order in which I put these two functions. They are in that order so as to emphasize the point which Dr. Runyon made in chapter 6: "Meaning emerges from meaningful experience." Experience precedes meaning. Thus the clergyman's task is to help a person understand his experience and to be the midwife to fresh experiencing. Then he can assist in the mining operation. When the presentation of the biblical story is only a trip to the Holy Land in a day that's gone, or when someone merely stirs up the ancient dust of history, there is little meaning. That is not the biblical theologian's task. Rather it is for him to be available, to be a pointer, to be a guide to treasures which can illumine what has already happened; and he can be a guide because his own life is illumined by that history.

Policy Implication. Religious leaders need to be trained in group process. They are already trained as biblical theologians, but need help in integrating the Word and this new world of experiencing and helping: this should be a major goal in the continuing education of the clergy. Word integration should be *the* major effort in lay theological education. Biblical theologians who can give training in the art of loving can also fulfill the most valuable function of helping modern church members find their experiences illumined by the biblical story.

IV. CELEBRATION

Hypothesis. New concepts (understandings) of celebration

can emerge from an analysis of the experiences of Shalom Retreats.

Result. Because in chapter 8 we have made an analysis of the celebrative experiences of our Shalom Retreats and have isolated the operant principles, here we simply refer to those principles and seek to isolate policy implications.

In most of our churches today modern man is worshiping in the forms of the past, using language and belief systems more readily acceptable in the past than in the present, singing hymns which contain images, ideas, and affirmations which no longer are directly related to man's present experiencing. Many people are content and not only conform to this condition but are warmed by it and comforted and even inspired. But there are many more today who simply cannot go along. They know that modern man, just as his forbears did, must develop his own forms, his own ways of confessing his faith, his own way of celebrating. They find the church without ecstasy, tepid, formal, and bland. We speak on behalf of these and say that religious leaders need to be midwives to the birthing of the new so that modern man may worship in meaningful categories and according to his experiencing.

The next section will deal with the importance of pluralism and the necessity to be sensitive to the polarizations in the church today.

During this interim period it is probably necessary to worship in our churches in different ways—in old forms with those who are still comfortable in them, and in new forms for those who are related to the church but no longer get satisfaction, encouragement, comfort, or joy out of old ways of worship.

Aware of the fact that the new is struggling to be born, many religious leaders today are tinkering with the old forms; but the result often is only that they destroy the order and rhythm of the old and impose upon the congregation a kind of chaos without order or rhythm, leaving the lovers of the old upset and those hungry for the new unsatisfied.

The old forms of worship are controlled by the clergy and sanctioned by the "leading laity." The experience is closely bound from the point of view of time—one hour. Everything is supposed to happen between the call to worship and the benediction, and exactly what is to happen is foreknown. To this extent it is designed as a nonhappening; the unexpected is kept to a bare minimum. Participation of the laity is closely controlled and their contribution largely limited to singing, silent prayer, and stated responses. Such rigidity tends to lack spontaneity, joy, celebration.

The new cannot be born unless worship leaders are willing to give up control, willing to trust process, willing to let the unexpected happen. This does not mean that no preparations are made. Careful preparation must be made to create the procelebrative conditions. (We can set up conditions for real celebration, or we can set up nonexpectant conditions.) But preparation does not include determining what will happen. Furthermore, without prior involvement of the people, without real meeting, there can be no great celebration. Celebration cannot rise higher than the relation of the people engaged in the celebration.

Policy Implication. Religious leaders need to be given training in creative worship and in the art of giving up control (sharing leadership).

V. RELATIONSHIP OF HUMAN POTENTIAL METHODS TO THE LOCAL CHURCH

Hypothesis. Persons "turned on" in these experiences can significantly affect the life of their local church.

Result. The instructions relative to theological reflection on the retreats included this suggestive question *Do you think these methods would work in the local church?* The question was offered among other questions to stimulate the imagination of the retreatants in doing their writing. 52% of the clergy and 63% of the laity answered the question (Kirkridge only). Of this number, 81% of the clergy and 70% of the laity said "Yes." In the follow-up four to ten months later we found that 76% of the clergy and 65% of the laity (Kirkridge and LaForet Groups combined) suggested the formation of small groups in which basic encounter methods would be central. Of this number 65% of the clergy and 34% of the laity said they were now in such groups. 65% of the clergy and 70% of the laity said that these groups were church-related.

Further, we asked the retreatants, "When you returned home did you suggest similar free worship services?" 90% of the clergy and 57% of the laity said "Yes." Of this number 75% of the persons said that their suggestion had been followed; 58% of the laity reported that their suggestions had been taken seriously and that some form of experimentation had been tried out.

Policy Implication. Policy-makers at all church levels should sanction and encourage research and training of church leaders, clergy, and laity in this field. The evidence though incomplete is strong that not only persons but the local church can be profoundly affected by the Human Potential Movement. But as Bonhoeffer said, "We will never know what we do not do."

But even as we make the policy recommendation we know that as this movement grows it will have rough sledding in the church. It is experience-based, produces some "true believers," is threatening to what is. So even though policy-makers are "wise as serpents and harmless as doves" there are stormy times ahead. Yet because of the high promise, the way ahead is through the storm. The church can and will learn from this movement.

The American society today is polarized. Conflict is at an all time high. Churches reflect what is going on in the culture and accordingly are themselves conflict-laden and polarized. The chances of this situation improving in the near future are not good. But the church by taking a new stance can improve and enrich its own life and thereby be a help and a strength to the lives of the people who make up its life, and possibly a model for other institutions.

Policy Implication. That the church move away from a homogeneous, enclosed, and closed model to the pluralistic model of an open arena.

Most of our Protestant churches are built on the principle of homogeneity in class, color, and even perspective on the world. A high implied value is the absence of conflict: "Don't rock the boat." The agreeable is lifted up, the disagreeable hidden as far as possible. Thus valuing homogeneity, we encourage dishonesty in relations, a low level of sharing and thus a low level of learning from one another. In honoring pluralism we would come to see conflict not as an evil but as a means of going forward, a way of sharing and learning. Creative handling of conflict would become one of the necessary skills of religious leaders and would therefore have an indisputable place in cleric and laic theological education.

The pluralistic model of the church would visualize the church as a center of religious pilgrimage and therefore of continuous, unending "education." Here a person could go to receive help for his own journey, could be with like-minded souls from whom he could learn and with whom he would plan and act out ways of making a better world; could receive continuous illumination on his journey from the biblical story. Here in the church he would meet and encounter those who see the world in different ways, different from his—indeed, who might be opposed to his strategy for making a better world, even feel that helping to make a better world is not an essential or even a proper task of religion. But as covenanted members of the Judeo-Christian stream of history-making they would worship together and hear a pastor (biblical theologian), open up meanings of the story in terms of the present time. All could worship as a people honoring each other's right to think and feel individually, uniquely, and to make unique contributions to the common life.

The new ingredient here is the *open arena* model. In a church honoring pluralism and seeing conflict as potentially creative, people could gather regularly in the open arena to witness to one another, debate perspectives and strategies, learn from each other but at the same time act out the Christian understanding of the nature of love.

Under this model people would meet at the church, form their own task groups at the church, go to carry out their action in the world, come back into the church in the open arena to witness, agitate, and encourage others. They would act as Christians in the world, but they would not be able to say we are the church in action unless they were so authorized. Possibly other groups opposing them might go from the same church. But always there is the open arena to come back to where the speaking and the hearing may go on, where people honor each other by recognizing the right of each to think and feel as he does.

The religious leader here, as suggested by the section on community building, has the function of biblical theologian (illuminating the present in terms of the ancient story).

Under this model all kinds of groups could flourish. Those

who wish to continue to meet in safe small groups or none at all would do so. But there would also be those who wished to meet in intensive encounter groups, those who wished to develop groups in which intimacy, threat, and risk and were predominant, and growth in the art of loving would not be discouraged.

The contribution which the methods of the Human Potential Movement can make lie in providing process skills in community building. Without these skills the church may soon find itself in even more of a wilderness, increasingly homogeneous, torn by conflict, increasingly small, increasingly ineffective.

A SHALOM POSTSCRIPT

Shalom is a comprehensive word which in many ways defies description. Its fundamental meaning in the Old Testament is totality, well being, harmony. It is the untrammeled, free growth of the soul, harmonious community, every form of happiness and free expansion. It includes every kind of good for man, peace, justice, bodily health, long life of happiness ending in natural death. All these things and more and its heart and center is community with others, the foundation of life. In short it is all of the possible blessings God intends for man. This concept of what God intends is born in the Old Testament and is fully incorporated in the New. Thus it is both a Jewish and Christian concept.

In calling our retreats Shalom Retreats we intended the full, rich meaning of that concept. We are deeply concerned for the welfare and release of potential of the individual person, but we are as deeply concerned about the unjust structures of the world which imprison millions of the poor and alienated and which prevent Shalom for them. Thus we are concerned that the Human Potential Movement not be a means whereby the church moves toward isolation but rather is empowered to take its place in helping a new world to be born.

Our retreats utilize methods which are aimed at change and the release of human potential. We have demonstrated that this change and this release are possible. But now we wish to make this caveat: we are not simply interested in the individual, nor do we naively believe that by changing the individual you change the unjust structures of the world. This is the backwater into which a very promising movement, the Oxford

Group movement, was pushed. Thus Walter Houston Clark says:

> The central focus of Group endeavor is the "changed" life. "Change" is simply the Group term for conversion, the reorientation of the individual toward a better life. The Group sees its world mission in terms of changing people rather than in changing political situations, the social structure, or economic systems. This is one cardinal issue on which the group differs from Communism. But this also tends to separate the Groupist from fellow Christians who emphasize the Social Gospel as well as from the typical liberal and the non-communist socialist. This also helps to explain why the Oxford Group readily finds a warm spot in the hearts of many conservatives and those whose vested interests lie in the preservation of the *status quo.*[7]

We are not very much interested in the status quo, for it is bad news to untold millions of God's children all over the world. We are interested in a new world being born, in the family of man, and believe that the church has an important part to play in the birthing of a world where all shall have enough and be free from the curse of war, where God's intended Shalom shall not be for the fortunate few but for the many in the family of man. Human Potential methods employed by the church can, we believe, help to change its style of life and release persons in new ways to use their energies toward that better world.

A pastor very active in the social action field attended our most recent retreat in December 1970. He found new strength and vision and was surprised by joy. In his theological reflection at the end of the retreat he wrote a paeon of praise to God, a call and admonition to the church. We began this book with a word to the churches from a retreatant. What better way to end it than to include a portion of another retreatant's ecstatic reflection:

> This is the Lord's doing, and I praise Him in my amazement!
> Come and behold, O creation, and rejoice!
> For amazing grace has touched this earth, Emmanuel.
> Let the stars shine anew;
> Let the galaxies shed their light upon this great, new and wondrous thing;

---

[7]Walter Houston Clark, *The Oxford Group* (New York: Twayne Publishers, 1951), p. 27.

Let the universe continue to expand into the outer reaches
That this message and the Lord's song may be heard
Where they have not heard it before.
Sing, O winged birds; and let your songs convey Good News.
Let the oceans roll in pounding rocky shores,
Caressing the shoreline, creating new shapes
Forming new eddies through which the waters of life flow,
Cutting new channels, where none existed before.
New shapes are emerging, new patterns are being formed—
The old must give way. But don't be sad
For life is creative, dynamic—ever renewing itself.
Listen, O Church, let the ocean of God's love wash over you.
Do not prevent it; do not build your protective barriers against God's love.
To remain the same is to stagnate and the aroma you give off is putrid.
Be baptized afresh with the life-giving streams of water, let the tide roll in.
Don't hold it back; because if you do not open your doors and windows
That the waters may flow through, the waves will batter against your wall
Until they buckle and your devastation will be the judgement
That you were not prepared for your time of visitation.
Do not look to your wisemen to unlock your sacred and protected chambers.
Look to the simple, the free . . . to those who have lost their need to protect.
O child born in a stable, amidst the dung heaps of the stable,
We look for you where the rhythm of life and death is ever going on.
Will the wisemen know enough where to search out your presence in our midst?
Will a new star shine? Yes! Yes! Yes!
I believe, for light has shined for me and the sounds of nature tell the secret.
I hear . . . for the screams of the hurt, the pained, the angry vibrate with life
And beneath it all there is joy unbelievable.
I believe because I have been allowed to see and hear. Alleluia. Amen.

APPENDIX A
Retreat Materials

Letter sent to participants before the retreat:

KIRKRIDGE SHALOM RETREATS
29 Overhill Road Scarsdale, N.Y. 10583

We are delighted that you will participate in the Shalom Retreat at Kirkridge. It will be a memorable experience for all of us, an experience in which we will all grow and celebrate together. The purpose of this letter is to mention a few important matters relative to the retreat.

Enclosed we send you a map which should help you find Kirkridge. Please note that we will be staying at the Lodge which is located on the Appalachian Trail, about ½ mile from Route 191, halfway between Bangor and Stroudsburg.

It is very important that we be able to eat at 7 o'clock. We encourage you to get to Kirkridge as early as you can. An hour or so of sitting "loose in the saddle" will help. We are hopeful that everyone will indeed be present for dinner and remember, our covenant is to remain until the end of the retreat.

Should you find yourself all of a sudden unable to come to the retreat then please notify us immediately (Tel. 914-472-2493). If you plan to travel by public transportation then please call Mrs. John Nelson (Jane) at Kirkridge (Tel. 215-581-5078) at least by noon on Wednesday so that you can be met at Allentown Airport or the Stroudsburg bus depot.

We suggest you wear your most comfortable clothing since we will be sitting around a lot, mostly on the floor. We strongly discourage the use of liquor and drugs because they easily hinder us from being fully present to each other. If you are presently in psychotherapy or have a history of heart trouble then we will need your therapist's or physician's OK for you to participate in the retreat.

The telephone number at the Lodge is 215-581-5078. We are sure that none of us wish to receive phone calls during the course of the retreat but it will probably be a comfort to you to leave the number behind in case that you must be reached.

We enclose another copy of the brochure. Please read it again carefully as it will help you get oriented before you come to the retreat.

We are much looking forward to being with you. SHALOM!

(signed) Jerry and Elisabeth

Letter sent to participants after the retreat:

Dear__________________________,

One of our great joys during the past year was sharing with you in a Shalom Retreat. We have found our lives greatly enriched and see increasingly great possibilities in the human potential movement. As you know we are writing a book about the Human Potential Movement. It will contain our hopes and what we have learned in our Shalom Retreats.

Now we are asking for your help. Will you please fill out the enclosed questionnaire, take the Firo-B test again and return them both to us as soon as possible.

Since we are particularly interested to know whether the Shalom Retreats initiate "behavioral change that sticks," we are seeking also data from significant others related to our retreatants. Thus, we are asking you also to have a significant other answer our questions shown on a separate sheet.

We are much aware that we are asking a lot of you. We dare to do it because we have good reasons to believe that you also see great possibilities in this movement and want to see it continued.

We send you our love and hope that all is well with you.
Shalom!

Jerry and Elisabeth
GJJ/EJ/rm

FOLLOW-UP QUESTIONNAIRE:
(to be filled out by significant other)

We are conducting research relative to the Shalom Retreats which we lead. These retreats rely very heavily upon basic encounter as the essential method and we pay careful attention to feelings of fear, pain and anger as blocks to the free expression of love and joy.

You are closely acquainted with the person who gave you this questionnaire, a person who participated in a Shalom Retreat. As part of our research relative to behavioral change we ask you to fill out this questionnaire. It will not take a great deal of time on your part and will be of inestimable value to us. Please use the enclosed addressed and stamped envelope to return your reply to us. Thank you.

Jerry and Elisabeth Jud
Retreat-leaders

Do you think the behavior of ________________________ was affected significantly as a result of (his/her) experience at a Shalom Retreat?

Yes____ no____

Do you consider this change ____positive or ____negative?

Please describe the changed behavior as you perceive it.

We would like you to sign this questionnaire. Please indicate what your relationship is to the person about whom you have given the above information.

______________________ Signature

______________________ relationship

FOLLOW-UP QUESTIONNAIRE
(to be filled out by retreatant)

It will be of great help to us in our research if you will kindly fill out this questionnaire. Please be as honest as you can. You may find it helpful to read the entire questionnaire before beginning your answers.

I. Personal Data

1. *Name*
2. *Age*
3. *Profession*
4. *Marital Status:*
   a. ____*single*
   b. ____*married*
   c. ____*separated*
   d. ____*divorced*
   e. ____*widowed*
5. *With whom did you attend the Shalom Retreat? (Please check all that apply)*
   a. ____*spouse*
   b. ____*friend*
   c. ____*alone*
   d. ____*people from your church*
6. *Prior to the Shalom Retreat, did you have sensitivity training or encounter experience? yes____ no____*

II. Behavioral Change

7. *In which of the following areas do you express your needs or your feelings more than you did before the Shalom Retreat?*
   a. ____*need to be loved*
   b. ____*love for others*
   c. ____*anger*
   d. ____*pain*
   e. ____*fear*
   f. ____*joy*
   g. ____*other (please explain)*
   h. ____*none of the above*
8. Immediately *after the Shalom Retreat, did you notice a change in your feelings*
   a. *toward yourself? yes____ no____ (please describe)*
   b. *toward significant others (e.g. your spouse, your children, close friend)? yes____ no____ (please describe)*
   c. *toward other people (e.g. colleagues at work, friends, neighbors) yes____ no____ (please describe)*
9. *Do you* continue *to feel differently*
   a. *toward yourself? yes____ no____*
   b. *toward significant others? yes____ no____*
   c. *toward other people? yes____ no____*
10. *Do you consider yourself more sensitive now to the needs and problems of the world? yes____ no____*
    If yes, please describe

III. Local Church Relationships

11. *Are you related to a local church?* *yes____ no____*

Please Note: If You Answer Question 11 in the Negative You May Skip to Question 18

12. *Are you*
    a. ____*layman*
    b. ____*clergyman, D.R.E.*
    c. ____*clergyman's wife*
    d. ____*church executive*
    e. ____*officer in your church (e.g. deacon, trustee, Sunday School teacher)*

13. If you are a layman
    a. *was your attitude toward your pastor affected by the Shalom Retreat? yes____ no____*
       1) *if yes, please describe this change in attitude*
       2) *have you expressed this directly to him? yes____ no____*

14. *If you are a clergyman,*
    a. *was your attitude toward your congregation affected by the Shalom Retreat? yes____ no____*
       1) *If yes, please describe this change in attitude*
       2) *have you expressed this directly to some members of your church? yes____ no____*

15. *As a result of the Shalom Retreat, do you find it*
    a. ____*easier*
    b. ____*same as before*
    c. ____*more difficult*

    to accept the present state of the institutional church?

16. *Have you discussed these feelings with*
    a. ____*other members of your church?*
    b. ____*your pastor?*

17. *Have you since the Shalom Retreat*
    a. *suggested freer forms of celebration (worship)? yes____ no____*
    b. *if yes, were your suggestions followed through? yes____ no____*

18. *Have you since the Shalom Retreat*
    a. *suggested or initiated any type of small group in which basic encounter methods are central? yes____ no____*
    b. *if yes, did you do this within the church? yes____ no____*

19. *Are you at the present time*
    a. *participating in such a group? yes____ no____*
    b. *if yes, is this group related to the church? yes____ no____*

20. *What significance did the celebration at the Shalom Retreat have for you personally?*

21. *Has the Shalom Retreat had a lasting effect on your understanding of*
    a. *the meaning of life or your religion? yes____ no____*
       if yes, please describe
    b. *the mission of the church? yes____ no____*
       if yes, please describe

IV. Counseling

22. *Have you within the past five years received professional help such as extended counseling with a pastor or psychotherapist?*
    yes____ no____

23. *Were you in counseling/therapy at the time of the Shalom Retreat?*
    yes____ no____

24. *Are you at the present time in counseling/therapy?*
    yes______ no______

25. *Did you begin counseling as a result of the Shalom Retreat?*
    yes____ no____

26. *Did you terminate counseling/therapy as a result of the Shalom Retreat?*
    yes____ no____

27. *This space is for you to use—just in case you want to say something more.*

APPENDIX B

Statistical Tables

TABLE A1

Time-Span Between Retreat and Follow-up Study (Kirkridge Group Only)

Months	4	5	6	7	8	9	10	Mean: 6 months
Number retreatants	43	12	13	16	12	9	10	Total no.: 115
Percentage	37.5	10.4	11.3	13.9	10.4	7.8	8.7	100%

TABLE A2

Return of Questionnaire

	Kirkridge		LaForet		Albright	
	%	No.	%	No.	%	No.
Not returned	8.7	10	11.4	4	17.6	3
Returned	91.3	105	88.6	31	82.4	14

TABLE A3

Age

	Kirkridge		LaForet		Albright	
	%	No.	%	No.	%	No.
-19					35.7	5
20-29	9.5	10	16.1	5	64.3	9
30-39	43.8	46	48.4	15		
40-49	31.4	33	16.1	5		
50-59	11.4	12	19.4	6		
60-	3.8	4				
	100.0	105	100.0	31	100.0	14

TABLE A4

Sex

	Kirkridge		LaForet		Albright	
	%	No.	%	No.	%	No.
Men	47.6	50	71	22	42.9	6
Women	52.4	55	29	9	57.1	8
	100.0	105	100.0	31	100.0	14

TABLE A5

Marital Status

	Kirkridge		LaForet		Albright	
	%	No.	%	No.	%	No.
Married	86.7	91	100.0	31		
Single	6.7	7			100.0	14
Separated	1.9	2				
Divorced	3.8	4				
Widowed	1	1				
	100.1	105	100.0	31	100.0	14

TABLE A6

Geographical Distribution

	Kirkridge		LaForet		Albright	
	%	No.	%	No.	%	No.
New York	34.3	36	6.5	2		
Pennsylvania	15.2	16			100.0	14
Metropolitan Washington	14.3	15				
South & Southwest	8.6	9	6.5	2		
New England	8.6	9	6.5	2		
New Jersey	7.6	8				
Midwest	5.7	6	67.7	21		
Canada	5.7	6				
West & Northwest			12.9	4		
	100.0	105	100.0	31	100.0	14

TABLE A7

With Whom Did They Come to the Retreat?

	Kirkridge		LaForet		Albright	
	%	No.	%	No.	%	No.
With spouse	68.6	72	51.6	16		
Alone	15.2	16	48.4	15		
With friend	16.2	17			100.0	14
	100.0	105	100.0	31	100.0	14

TABLE A8

Previous Sensitivity Training

	Kirkridge		LaForet		Albright	
	%	No.	%	No.	%	No.
No answer	1.9	2				
No	42.9	45	48.4	15	85.7	12
Yes	55.2	58	51.6	16	14.3	2
	100.0	105	100.0	31	100.0	14

TABLE A9

Long-term Counseling

	Kirkridge		LaForet		Albright	
	%	No.	%	No.	%	No.
During 5 years preceding retreat	28.6	29	12.9	4		none
At time of retreat	15.2	16	3.2	1		none
Started since retreat	2.9	3		none		none
Terminated since retreat	4.8	5		none		none

TABLE A10

Church Membership

	Kirkridge		LaForet		Albright	
	%	No.	%	No.	%	No.
No answer					7.1	1
Not members	7.6	8			28.6	4
Members	92.4	97	100.0	31	64.3	9
	100.0	105	100.0	31	100.0	14

TABLE A11

Denominational Affiliation

Kirkridge Group

	%	No.		%	No.
United Church of Christ	34.3	36	Friends' Meeting	1.9	2
Presbyterian	18.1	19	Unitarian	1.9	2
Baptist	9.5	10	Lutheran	1.0	1
Methodist	5.7	6	Mennonite	1.0	1
United Church of Canada	5.7	6	Unknown	2.9	3
Episcopal	2.9	3	Nonmembers	7.6	8
Church of the Saviour	2.9	3		100.0	105
Reformed Church	1.9	2			

TABLE A12

Position in Church

	Kirkridge		LaForet	
	%	No.	%	No.
Layman	27.6	29	6.5	2
Clergy	20.0	21	64.5	20
Clergy wife	14.3	15	22.5	7
Church executive	2.9	3	6.5	2
Church officer (trustee, deacon, Sunday school teacher)	27.6	29		
Nonmembers	7.6	8		
	100.0	105	100.0	31

TABLE A13

Expression of Need for Love,
Love for Others, Anger
Laity Versus Clergy
(Kirkridge and LaForet Groups)

	Need for Love		Love for Others		Anger	
	%	No.	%	No.	%	No.
Laity (95)	70.5	67	78	32	**55.8**	53
Clergy (41)	75.6	31	77.9	74	**75.6**	31

TABLE A14

Expression of Need for Love,
Love for Others, Anger
Men of Other Professions Versus Clergy
(Kirkridge Group Only)

	Need for Love		Love for Others		Anger	
	%	No.	%	No.	%	No.
Other men (29)	**66.7**	18	81	17	33.3	9
Clergy (21)	**95.2**	20	77.8	21	81	17

TABLE A15

Expression of Positive, Positive + Negative, or Only Negative Feelings

	Kirkridge %	Kirkridge No.	LaForet %	LaForet No.	Albright %	Albright No.
Positive	25.7	27	9.7	3	14.3	2
Positive + Negative	**64.7**	**68**	**83.9**	**26**	**71.4**	**10**
Negative	5.7	6	6.5	2	14.3	2
Neither	3.8	4				
	99.9	105	100.1	31	100.0	14

TABLE A16

Immediate Change in Feelings Toward Self

	Kirkridge %	Kirkridge No.	LaForet %	LaForet No.	Albright %	Albright No.
No change	8.6	9	3.2	1		
Change	**91.4**	96	**96.8**	30	**100.0**	14
	100.0	105	100.0	31	100.0	14

TABLE A17

Immediate Change in Feelings Toward Significant Other

	Kirkridge %	Kirkridge No.	LaForet %	LaForet No.	Albright %	Albright No.
No answer	1.9	2			7.1	1
No change	5.7	6	3.2	1		
Change	**92.4**	97	**96.8**	30	**92.9**	13
	100.0	105	100.0	31	100.0	14

TABLE A18

Immediate Change in Feelings Toward Others

	Kirkridge		LaForet		Albright	
	%	No.	%	No.	%	No.
No answer	1	1				
No change	9.5	10	6.5	2	not asked	
Change	**89.5**	94	**93.5**	29		
	100.0	105	100.0	31		

TABLE A19

Return of Confidential Evaluation

	Kirkridge		LaForet		Albright	
	%	No.	%	No.	%	No.
Not returned	5.7	6	29	9	28.6	4
Returned	**94.3**	99	**71**	22	**71.4**	10
	100.0	105	100.0	31	100.0	14

TABLE A20

Relationship of Evaluator to Retreatant

	Kirkridge		LaForet		Albright	
	%	No.	%	No.	%	No.
Spouse	65.6	65	72.7	16		
Friend	27.3	27	27.3	6	100.0	10
Relative	7.1	7				
	100.0	99	100.0	22	100.0	10

TABLE A21

Change of Behavior as Reported by Significant Other

	Kirkridge		LaForet		Albright	
	%	No.	%	No.	%	No.
No Change	11.2	11	4.6	1	20	2
Change	**88.8**	88	**95.4**	21	**80**	8
	100.0	99	100.0	22	100	10

TABLE A22

Total Scores on FIRO-B (in percentages of total N)

	Kirkridge (N = 105)				Albright (N = 14)			
	Low	Med.	High	N.A.*	Low	Med.	High	N.A.*
Test I	21.9	44.4	33.3	—	28.6	21.4	50	—
Test II	9.5	41	46.7	2.9	14.3	28.6	50	7.1

*N.A. stands for "no answer." A few persons did not return the second test or did not complete it.

	Change Test I—Test II								
	Ups	Downs	Same	L-M	L-H	M-H	M-L	H-M	H-L
Kirkridge	37.2	13.4	46.7	**12.4**	3.8	**21**	2.9	7.6	2.9
Albright	21.4	14.3	57.1	7.1	—	**14.3**	—	**14.3**	—

First, an explanation of the lower set of tables, those referred to as "Change Test I—Test II."

Ups: *combined upward changes* from one level to a higher one; includes all three of the following:
L-M low to medium
L-H low to high
M-H medium to high
Downs: *combined downward changes* from one level to a lower one; includes all three of the following:
M-L medium to low
H-M high to medium
H-L high to low
Same: *includes scores that remained at the same level,* i.e., all the ones that remained at low, medium, and high levels combined.

Percentage figures in bold face exceed 10 percent and are particularly important (see quote from Schutz on page 87).

TABLE A23

Comparison of Total Scores— Men and Women (K-Group)

	Men (50)				Women (55)			
	Low	Med.	High	N.A.	Low	Med.	High	N.A.
Test I	22	36	42	—	8	38	52	2
Test II	21.8	52.7	25.5	—	10.9	43.6	41.8	3.6

	Change Test I—Test II									
	Ups	Downs	Same	L-M	L-H	M-H	M-L	H-M	H-L	N.A.
Men	38	14	46	**14**	4	**20**	2	10	2	2
Women	36.3	12.7	47.3	10.9	3.6	**21.8**	3.6	5.5	3.6	3.6

TABLE A24

Comparison of Total Scores—
Married Persons Versus
Persons Without Spouse (K-Group)

	Married (91)				Without spouse (14)			
	Low	Med.	High	N.A.	Low	Med.	High	N.A.
Test I	25	43.8	31.3		21.3	44.9	33.7	
Test II	—	31.3	62.5	6.3	11.2	42.7	43.8	2.2

	Change Test I—Test II									
	Ups	Downs	Same	L-M	L-H	M-H	M-L	H-M	H-L	N.A.
Married	62.6	6.3	25	**18.8**	6.3	**37.5**	—	6.3	—	6.3
Without spouse	32.6	14.7	50.6	**11.2**	3.4	**18**	3.4	7.9	3.4	2.2

TABLE A25

Inclusion Scores
(Kirkridge and Albright Groups)

	Kirkridge (105)				Albright (14)			
	Low	Med.	High	N.A.	Low	Med.	High	N.A.
Test I	48.6	18.1	33.3	—	28.6	14.3	57.1	—
Test II	30.5	16.2	50.5	2.9	14.3	21.4	57.1	7.1

	Change Test I—Test II									
	Ups	Downs	Same	L-M	L-H	M-H	M-L	H-M	H-L	N.A.
Kirkridge	36.2	12.4	48.6	9.5	**18.1**	8.6	3.8	1.9	6.7	2.9
Albright	21.4	21.4	50	—	7.1	**14.3**	—	**21.4**	—	7.1

TABLE A26

Inclusion Scores—
Men and Women (K-Group)

	Men (50)				Women (55)			
	Low	Med.	High	N.A.	Low	Med.	High	N.A.
Test I	4.6	12	42	—	50.9	23.6	25.5	—
Test II	20	20	50	2	37.7	12.7	50.9	3.6

	Change Test I—Test II									
	Ups	Downs	Same	L-M	L-H	M-H	M-L	H-M	H-L	N.A.
Men	38	16	44	**14**	**18**	6	2	4	10	2
Women	34.6	9.1	52.7	5.5	**18.2**	10.9	5.5	—	3.6	3.6

TABLE A27

Control Scores
(Kirkridge and Albright Groups)

	Kirkridge (105)				Albright (14)			
	Low	Med.	High	N.A.	Low	Med.	High	N.A.
Test I	24.8	41	34.3	—	21.4	42.9	35.7	—
Test II	28.6	41	27.6	2.9	35.7	35.7	21.4	7.1

	Change Test I—Test II									
	Ups	Downs	Same	L-M	L-H	M-H	M-L	H-M	H-L	N.A.
Kirkridge	19.1	25.8	53.3	8.6	3.8	6.7	**12.4**	9.5	2.9	2.9
Albright	7.1	42.9	42.9	7.1	—	—	**28.6**	4.3	—	7.1

TABLE A28

Control Scores—
Men and Women (K-Group)

	Men (50)				Women (55)			
	Low	Med.	High	N.A.	Low	Med.	High	N.A.
Test I	18	40	42	—	30.9	41.8	27.3	—
Test II	30	36	32	2	27.3	45.5	23.6	3.6

	Change Test I—Test II									
	Ups	Downs	Same	L-M	L-H	M-H	M-L	H-M	H-L	N.A.
Men	14	32	52	4	2	8	14	**16**	2	2
Women	23.7	18.1	54.5	**12.7**	5.5	5.5	10.9	3.6	3.6	3.6

TABLE A29

Control Scores—
Pastors and Men of Other Professions (K-Group)

	Pastors (21)				Other Men (27)			
	Low	Med.	High	N.A.	Low	Med.	High	N.A.
Test I	14.3	28.6	57.1		18.5	51.9	29.6	—
Test II	38.1	28.6	28.6	4.8	25.9	40.7	33.3	—

	Change Test I—Test II									
	Ups	Downs	Same	L-M	L-H	M-H	M-L	H-M	H-L	N.A.
Pastors	4.8	47.6	42.9	4.8	—	—	**23.8**	**19**	4.8	4.8
Other men	18.5	22.2	59.3	—	3.7	**14.8**	7.4	**14.8**	—	—

TABLE A30

Affection Scores
(Kirkridge and Albright Groups)

	Kirkridge (105)				Albright (14)			
	Low	Med.	High	N.A.	Low	Med.	High	N.A.
Test I	29.5	28.6	41.9	—	35.7	21.4	42.9	—
Test II	12.4	23.8	**61**	2.9	14.3	7.1	**71.4**	7.1

	Change Test I—Test II									
	Ups	Downs	Same	L-M	L-H	M-H	M-L	H-M	H-L	N.A.
Kirkridge	39.1	15.3	42.9	8.6	**12.4**	**18.1**	4.8	9.5	1	2.9
Albright	35.6	—	57.1	7.1	7.1	**21.4**	—	—	—	7.1

TABLE A31

Affection Scores—
Persons Without Spouse (K-Group)

	Married (91)				Without Spouse (14)			
	Low	Med.	High	N.A.	Low	Med.	High	N.A.
Test I	28.6	28.6	42.9	—	35.7	28.6	35.7	—
Test II	11	20.9	**64.8**	3.3	21.4	42.9	**35.7**	—

	Change Test I—Test II									
	Ups	Downs	Same	L-M	L-H	M-H	M-L	H-M	H-L	N.A.
Married	**40.7**	14.3	41.8	7.7	**13.2**	**19.8**	4.4	8.8	1.1	3.3
Without spouse	**28.5**	21.4	50	**14.3**	7.1	7.1	7.1	**14.3**	—	—

TABLE A32

Affection Scores—
Persons with Versus Persons Without
Previous Sensitivity Training (K-Group)

	With Previous Sensitivity Training (58)				No Previous Sensitivity Training (45)			
	Low	Med.	High	N.A.	Low	Med.	High	N.A.
Test I	31	25.9	43.1	—	28.9	33.3	37.8	—
Test II	12.1	19	**67.2**	1.7	13.3	31.1	**51.1**	4.4

	Change Test I—Test II									
	Ups	Downs	Same	L-M	L-H	M-H	M-L	H-M	H-L	N.A.
With	43.2	15.4	39.7	5.2	**19**	**19**	3.4	10.3	1.7	1.7
Without	35.5	15.6	44.4	**13.3**	4.4	**17.8**	6.7	8.9		4.4

TABLE A33

Affection Scores—
Pastors and Men of Other Professions (K-Group)

	Pastors (21)				Other Men (27)			
	Low	Med.	High	N.A.	Low	Med.	High	N.A.
Test I	19	38.1	**42.9**	—	37	18.5	**44.4**	—
Test II	14.83		**81**	4.8	11.1	29.6	**59.3**	—

	Change Test I—Test II									
	Ups	Downs	Same	L-M	L-H	M-H	M-L	H-M	H-L	N.A.
Pastors	47.6	9.6	38.1	—	**14.3**	**33.3**	4.8	—	4.8	4.8
Other men	44.4	18.5	37	**14.8**	**14.8**	**14.8**	3.7	**14.8**		

TABLE A34

FIRO-B Raw Scores

	Kirkridge		Control Group	Albright		Control Group
	Test I	Test II	I	Test I	Test II	II
Inclusion expressed	4.5	5.3	5.9	5.1	5.9	5.4
Inclusion wanted	4.3	3.1	4.6	6.1	6.5	4.0
Total inclusion	8.8	8.4	10.5	11.2	12.4	9.4
Control expressed	4.1	4.0	4.7	4.3	4.0	3.4
Control wanted	6.0	5.3	5.5	6.7	5.1	5.0
Total control	10.2	9.2	10.2	11.0	9.1	8.4
Affection expressed	4.2	5.6	4.4	4.2	5.7	3.6
Affection wanted	6.1	6.6	5.1	5.1	6.5	4.9
Total affection	10.3	12.2	9.5	9.4	12.2	8.5
Total of all three need areas	29.2	31.7	30.2	31.6	33.5	26.3

Control Group I: Educational administrators; N-104; men and women; ages 26-64
Control Group II: Psychology majors; N-35; men and women

TABLE A35

Effect of Retreat on Understanding of the Meaning of Life and Religion

	Clergy (41)		Laity (87)		Albright (14)	
	%	No.	%	No.	%	No.
No answer	—	—	—	—	7.1	1
No	9.8	4	16.1	14	7.1	1
Yes	**90.2**	37	**83.9**	73	**85.7**	12

TABLE A36

Effect of Retreat on Understanding of the Mission of the Church

	Clergy (41)		Laity (87)	
	%	No.	%	No.
No answer	2.4	1	—	—
No	9.8	4	28.7	25
Yes	**87.8**	36	**71.3**	62

TABLE A37

Acceptance of the Institution in Its Present State

	Clergy (41)		Laity (87)		Albright (14)	
	%	No.	%	No.	%	No.
No answer	2.4	1	5.8	5	7.1	1
Easier	31.7	13	6.9	6	21.4	3
Same as before	9.8	4	33.3	29	**14.3**	2
More difficult	**56.1**	23	**54.0**	47	57.1	8

TABLE A38

Discussion About Institutional Church with Other Members and/or Pastor of Church

	Clergy (41)		Clergy-wives (22)		Laity (65)	
	%	No.	%	No.	%	No.
No answer	12.2	5	22.8	5	16.9	11
With neither	4.9	2	4.5	1	6.1	4
With pastor					4.6	3
With pastor or fellow pastor and others	4.9	2	50.0	11	40.0	26
With others	78.0	32	22.8	5	32.3	21

TABLE A39

Change of Attitude of Laity and Clergy Toward Each Other and Expression of This Change in Attitude

	Clergy (41)		Laity* (65)	
	%	No.	%	No.
No answer	4.9	2	14.4	10
No change	7.3	3	40.0	26
Change	**87.8**	36	**45.6**	29
Change expressed	**88.8**	32	**65.6**	19

*Pastors' wives excluded.

TABLE A40

Suggestion for Freer Forms of Celebration (Worship) and Follow-through of Suggestion

	Clergy (41)		Laity (87)	
	%	No.	%	No.
No answer	2.4	1	8.9	8
No suggestion made	9.8	4	39.2	34
Suggestion made	**87.8**	36	**51.9**	45
Suggestion followed	**75.0**	27	**57.7**	26

TABLE A41

Suggestion of Small Groups—in Church—and Presently in Small Group—in Church

	Clergy (41)		Laity (95)*	
	%	No.	%	No.
Groups suggested	**61.0**	25	**35.8**	34
in church	71.4	15	73.3	22
Now in such group	**56.1**	23	**34.4**	31
in church	82.6	19	70.9	22

*Includes nonchurch members.

APPENDIX C

Centers Where Human Relations Experiences from a Christian Perspective Are Offered

Mid-Atlantic Training Committee Suite 325 1500 Massachusetts Avenue, NW Washington, D.C. 20005	The Rev. John Denham 202/223-4763
New England Training Institute 222 West Main Street Waterbury, Conn. 06702	The Rev. Ronald G. Kurtz 203/673-3996
Episcopal Diocese of Olympia 1551 Tenth Avenue East Seattle, Washington 98102	Mrs. Lynn Young 206/325-4200
Episcopal Diocese of Alabama Carpenter House 521 North 20th Street Birmingham, Alabama 35203	The Rev. William A. Yon 205/324-7639
Center for Creative Living and Spiritual Growth 2580 West Broad Street Athens, Georgia 30601	The Rev. Del R. Poling 404/548-3195
Lands End—Adult Study Center of the Presbyterian Synod of New York Star Route 109 Box 5 Saranac Lake, New York 12983	Mr. Newton S. Fink 518/891-4034
Naramata Centre for Continuing Education Naramata, B.C., Canada	The Rev. Ivan Cumming
Prairie Christian Training Centre Fort Qu'Appelle, Saskatchewan, Canada	The Rev. Bud Harper
Atlantic Christian Training Center Tatamagouche, N.S., Canada	The Rev. Bob Latimer

Board for Interdenominational Training in Ohio 412 Sycamore Street Cincinnati, Ohio 45202	Mrs. Dorothy Fletcher 513/421-0311
Central Pennsylvania Synod of the Lutheran Synod in America 900 South Arlington Avenue Harrisburg, Pa. 17109	Mrs. John M. Glant, III Mr. Ira Sassaman
Church of the Brethren—Human Relations Laboratory 1451 Dundee Avenue Elgin, Illinois 60120	
Institute for Advanced Pastoral Studies 380 Lone Pine Road Bloomfield Hills, Michigan 48013	313/646-9375
New York-New Jersey Training Committee Box 38 West Lake Road Cazenovia, New York 13035	The Rev. William Foreman 315/655-3123
National Council of the Churches of Christ Department of Education Development 475 Riverside Drive Room 714 New York, New York 10027	212/749-2200

BIBLIOGRAPHY

Bach, George R. and Deutsch, Ronald. *Pairing*. New York: Peter H. Wyden, 1970.

Bach, George R. and Wyden, Peter. *The Intimate Enemy*. New York: William Morrow, 1969.

Berne, Eric. *Games People Play*. New York: Grove Press, 1964.

———. *Transactional Analysis in Psychotherapy*. New York: Grove Press, 1961.

Bugental, James F., ed. *Challenges of Humanistic Psychology*. New York: McGraw-Hill, 1967.

Burton, Arthur, ed. *Encounter*. San Francisco: Jossey-Bass, 1969.

Clark, Walter Houston. *The Oxford Group*. New York: Twayne Publishers, 1951.

Cox, Harvey. *The Feast of Fools*. Cambridge, Mass.: Harvard University Press, 1969.

Fagan, Joen and Shepherd, Irma Lee, eds. *Gestalt Therapy Now*. Palo Alto, Calif.: Science & Behavior Books, 1969.

Frankl, Victor. *The Will to Meaning*. New York: New American Library, 1969.

Gunther, Bernard. *Sense Relaxation: Below Your Mind*. New York: Collier Books, 1968.

Gustaitis, Rasa. *Turning On*. New York: Macmillan, 1969.

Harris, Thomas A. *I'm Ok—You're Ok*. New York: Harper & Row, 1969.

Hodge, Marshall Bryant. *Your Fear of Love*. Garden City, N.Y.: Doubleday, 1967.

Howard, Jane. *Please Touch*. New York: McGraw-Hill, 1970.

Janov, Arthur. *The Primal Scream*. New York: G. P. Putnam's Sons, 1970.

Jourard, Sidney M. *The Transparent Self*. Princeton, N. J.: D. Van Nostrand, 1964.

Keen, Sam. *Apology for Wonder*. New York: Harper & Row, 1969.

———. *To a Dancing God*. New York: Harper & Row, 1970.

Leonard, George B. *Education and Ecstasy*. New York: Dell Publishing Co., 1968.

Lowen, Alexander. *The Betrayal of the Body*. New York: Macmillan, 1966.

Malamud, Daniel I. and Machover, Solomon. *Toward Self-Understanding: Group Techniques in Self-Confrontation*. Springfield, Ill.: Charles C. Thomas, 1965.

Maslow, Abraham H. *Toward a Psychology of Being*. Princeton, N. J.: D. Van Nostrand, 1962.

May, Rollo. *Love and Will*. New York: W. W. Norton & Co., 1969.

Mowrer, O. Hobart. *The Crisis in Psychiatry and Religion*. Princeton, N. J.: D. Van Nostrand, 1961.

———. *The New Group Therapy*. Princeton, N. J.: D. Van Nostrand, 1964.

O'Banion, Terry and O'Connell, April. *The Shared Journey*. Englewood Cliffs, N. J.: Prentice-Hall, 1970.

Otto, Herbert A. *Group Methods to Actualize Human Potential*. Beverly Hills, Calif.: Holistic Press.

———. *A Guide to Developing Your Potential*. New York: Charles Scribner's Sons, 1967.

Otto, Herbert A. and Mann, John, eds. *Ways of Growth*. New York: Viking Press, 1969.

Perls, Frederick S. *Gestalt Therapy Verbatim*. Lafayette, Calif.: Real People Press, 1969.

Reid, Clyde. *Groups Alive, Church Alive*. New York: Harper & Row, 1969.

Rogers, Carl R. *Carl Rogers on Encounter Groups*. New York: Harper & Row, 1970.

Schutz, William C. *The Interpersonal Underworld*. Palo Alto, Calif.: Science & Behavior Books, 1967.

———. *Joy: Expanding Human Awareness*. New York: Grove Press, 1967.

Shostrom, Everett L. *Man, the Manipulator*. Nashville: Abingdon Press, 1967.

DATE DUE
